Look, You're a Leader!

DAISY HEPBURN

*A New Look at
Servant-Leadership
for Women*

Regal Books

A Division of GL Publications
Ventura, California, U.S.A.

Rights for publishing this book in other languages are contracted by Gospel Literature International (GLINT) foundation. GLINT also provides technical help for the adaptation, translation, and publishing of Bible study resources and books in scores of languages worldwide. For further information, contact GLINT, Post Office Box 6688, Ventura, California 93006, U.S.A., or the publisher.

Published by Regal Books
A Division of GL Publications
Ventura, California 93006
Printed in U.S.A.

Library of Congress Cataloging in Publication Data

Hepburn, Daisy.
    Look, you're a leader!

    Bibliography: p.
    1. Christian leadership.   2. Women—Religious life.
I. Title
BV652.1.H45   1985   262'.15'088042   85-19637
ISBN 0-8307-1098-1

The author and publisher have sought to locate and secure permission to reprint copyright material in this book. If any such acknowledgments have been inadvertently omitted, the publisher would appreciate receiving the information so that proper credit may be given in future printings.

Dedication

Servant-leaders? So many have influenced my life. Let this book be for some of them with my love.

To Doris, my sister, a teacher by godly example.

To Emily, my sister, a Salvation Army soldier.

To Ruth, my sister, a compassionate people-helper.

To Jane, my sister, who like a farmer has patience in adversity.

To Winnie, my friend, a workman and a woman of the Word.

To Rosella, my prayer partner, a vessel for her Master's use.

To Torunn, my friend who serves the Lord with gladness.

To Joan Bay Klope, with my deep appreciation, for her editing skills, persistence and patience.

Contents

Are You a Servant-Leader?

SERVANT-LEADERSHIP IN THE '80s

The '80s is the Decade of the Woman.

There are now more women in the ranks of the employed than ever before and the numbers grow daily. Women are becoming executives in corporations and presidents of colleges, airline pilots and attorneys, mayors of great cities and athletic achievers at every level. Women are being challenged to participate in highly financed leadership training to improve their skills.

I am almost convinced that while many women have been thrust into these battles for "rights," others have lagged in assuming leadership responsibilities. How are Christian women supposed to react to all of this social change? More important, what does Jesus say about *greatness* and *leadership*? "Whoever wants to become great among you must be your servant" (Matt. 20:26, *NIV*).

How does the role of servanthood fit in with the new roles women are assuming? Have we been too much influenced by the world's ideas of success and leadership?

Women of Influence: Who Do You Think You Are?

I nearly drove off the road. I was on an ordinary trip to the market and had the cassette player turned way up, ready to hear some words of wisdom. But no sound—then *big* sound! As if to shock me into responsibility, the words of the woman speaker crashed through the traffic noise and the screech of brakes at the stop sign!

"God has given to men authority," Joy Dawson stated, "but He has given women influence!" Joy Dawson is the wife of the director of "Youth with a Mission" and has an effective teaching ministry of her own. She developed her theme by citing examples of biblical women and their influence on the men in their lives.

My mind turned back to the premise that a woman's influence is a gift from God—perhaps especially to our sex. Of course, men wield an influence too, but I had to agree with Joy Dawson. God has given women the power to mark lives powerfully!

Leadership is the theme of Chuck Swindoll's book, *Hand Me Another Brick*. In that book, based on the story of Nehemiah, Pastor Swindoll has defined leadership in one word: influence!

When I arrived home again from that shopping trip, I went to my *Living Bible* and reread the verses in Luke 22. This incident is recorded in the first three Gospels. The conversation in the Upper Room was prefaced by a request that Salome, the mother of James and John, had made on the long walk to Jerusalem.

"Lord, when you come into your kingdom, can my sons be right up there with you—close to you?"

It is not hard for us mothers of sons to understand her query, is it! Why, I have made a similar request of the Lord Jesus often in my prayers—"Please Lord, keep my dear ones just as close to you as they will allow!"

Jesus used this continuing topic to teach a revolutionary lesson in leadership.

Jesus said, "In this world the kings and great men order their slaves around, and the slaves have no choice but to like it! But among you, the one who serves you best will be your leader. Out in the world the master sits at the table and is served by his servants. But not here! For I am your servant" (Luke 22:25-27, TLB).

Jesus teaches that true servanthood is *leadership.*

Chuck Swindoll defines leadership as *influence.*

Joy Dawson says that God has gifted women with *influence.*

Can it be that we have been too long influenced by the world's definition of leadership? Are we intimidated by the connotation of power, administration and chairmanship? Have we missed the most important spiritual challenge? The Lord Jesus is calling us to influence our world! Each of us is to become a woman of influence by serving well.

Salt influences the stew. Yeast influences the flour. The salt or yeast is not noticed for itself, but enhances, contributes and piques interest.

Do you see that what you *are,* as well as what you *do,* is an *influence?*

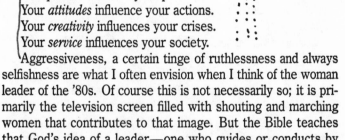

Your *kindness* influences your kids.
Your *humor* influences your home.
Your *joy* influences your job.
Your *peace* influences your problems.
Your *attitudes* influence your actions.
Your *creativity* influences your crises.
Your *service* influences your society.

Aggressiveness, a certain tinge of ruthlessness and always selfishness are what I often envision when I think of the woman leader of the '80s. Of course this is not necessarily so; it is primarily the television screen filled with shouting and marching women that contributes to that image. But the Bible teaches that God's idea of a leader—one who guides or conducts by showing the way—is a servant. Servant-leadership, appropriate for women's ministries, is a desperate need of the Church of Jesus Christ!

It will probably require a whole change of mindset, however. We will have to study the Word and discover new principles for leadership in order to serve, influence and guide.

It's Prime Time

Women in my age group—and let's not get too personal—the 40-60 age group (and even beyond!) are in *prime time.* We have just begun to recover from the shock of the empty-nest syndrome and we are more available for servant-leadership than ever before.

All sorts of changes have taken place in the Hepburn home. My husband is happier with less food, believe it or not. It is easier for me to keep house now than it has ever been. We have a strange second car that we lovingly refer to as The Bomb, but nevertheless find acceptable if not always dependable transportation. There are so many things that I am free to do now that even three or four years ago I was not free to do.

It's *prime time* for us women and surely God has the right to expect fruit through service from those of us who have been exposed for years to marvelous Bible studies, inspirational pulpit teaching and a veritable avalanche of Christian reading.

It's *prime time* and the local church can experience a new surge of vitality as God's women are willing to invest their strength and spiritual gifts in willing service—in *leadership*—based on the principles Jesus taught.

Let Me Introduce You

Consider your prime time for a moment. If someone were to describe you and your activities, what would they say? How would you *like* to be introduced?

This question was asked of me one day by the hostess of the women's luncheon to which I was about to speak. What a question! Dropping my eyes coyly, I mentioned a few little things she might want to say: wife, mother of two, washer of clothes, driver of car, regular church attender, etc. *But how would I like to be introduced?*

Can you imagine being an Olympic ski champion or the Pillsbury Bake-Off winner? Or Pulitzer Prize winner? Or a Super Mom? My imagination can run away with me. Wouldn't it be fun to be the great imposter for just a little while? I hear over and over again introductions that make me feel ordinary by comparison and I dream of being introduced as somebody extra-ordinary!

An Ordinary Adventure

My ordinariness is an embarrassment to me at times!

It was freezing cold when I pulled in to the parking lot and walked through the door of a local Christian radio station. Unaccustomed to being on the radio, the prospect of being interviewed held a kind of double fascination for me. It was only a 15-minute, Monday morning local program but I was delighted to be recorded on those marvelous ether airwaves and delighted at the fame that I was sure would result. Yes, there was a heady anticipation and excitement to the whole affair.

"I'm Daisy Hepburn and I have an appointment with Kaaren," I said to the young woman at the switchboard.

"Just a moment, dear," she said as she proceeded to call Kaaren. When Kaaren finally emerged from the inner office she proved to be one of those people who is entirely too good-looking for her own well-being! I was caught off guard to say the least. In a sweet tone she said, "Oh, Daisy! I'm so happy to meet you. Please just sit down and tell me all about yourself!" A leading question if I ever heard one.

"Well," I said, gulping, "what's to tell? We have two children or they have us, actually. I've been married to the same man for nearly 30 years—we've moved 16 or 18 times and—and—." I just couldn't think of anything noteworthy to say. Finally I sighed, "I guess you could just say that the Lord Jesus has led us through *an adventure in the ordinary.*"

Kaaren's face lit up. *"An adventure in the ordinary*—it's a great phrase and we'll use it on the air."

Before I could collect myself I was ushered into an inner sanctum, known in the trade as the taping studio, and given a seat behind a table. In front of me was a very large microphone. My eyes were drawn to the control booth where I saw a young man who appeared to be a life-sized replica of Winnie the Pooh. He began to signal with a smile and a series of gestures that it was time for us to begin. Kaaren listened for her cue as the music waned and said, "Good morning, ladies. We have with us today right here in our studio a lady who has lived *an adventure in the ordinary!* Tell us about it, Daisy Hepburn!"

What can I tell you? I sat there and was dumbstruck! I could not think of one single thing that was worth wafting out over those airwaves to the listening, waiting world. Not one thing seemed of sufficient value to share at that moment.

Well, I think I babbled on about my mother-in-law's coat and other tidbits that had little value. When the program engineer finally signaled that we were through, all I wanted to do was get out of there. Why had Kaaren invited me? Never have I felt so ordinary.

In her little book *Life Is Worth Living,* Betty Carlson says it so well when she tells of a wizened little elderly nun in Duluth giving a group of recent graduates some farewell words. With a wave she challenged them, "Remember, girls, never die of ordinariness!"

I am so thankful that our God did not plan for us to die of ordinariness or anonymity, but has given us special gifts, special abilities and special adventures.

How do you want to be introduced? How about an extraordinary woman of God!

I can think of dozens of great women of God—wouldn't it be fun to be introduced as one of them? However, I am old-shoe me. But just because I am rather ordinary by anyone's standard doesn't mean that the Lord does not have a unique place for me to fill. More than that, the Word of God challenges us to be willing to become all that God has in mind for us to be. That goal is nothing less than *excellence—perfection,* conformed exquisitely to the image of the Son of God Himself. Ordinary? Not for a minute!

In a world where women are demanding their rights, we find Scripture offering an alternative to this demand. By accepting responsibility and even further, living in submission to the plan of God and His shaping process, we become great through *servant-hood.* How I would like to be introduced as a great servant of the living God! Now that's a definition of a leader; one that is antithetical to the world's idea.

Portraits of Leadership

Paul, in 2 Timothy 2, depicts a gallery of portraits of the multi-faceted leader. Each one has leadership characteristics and functions that provide a study in equipping us to be servant-leaders according to God's design. I think I would like to be introduced as any one of the models Paul describes: As a *teacher* (v. 2) who accepts the responsibility of teaching the truth to others; as a *soldier* (vv. 3-4) who is willing to put on the whole armor of God and to do battle with sin; as an *athlete* (v. 5) who has a goal worth striving for and continually practices for the competition; as a *farmer* (v. 6) who is patient and willing to risk everything for the sake of a productive harvest; as a *workman* (v. 15) who is industrious and follows directions in order to build; as a *vessel* (vv. 20-21) who is cleansed and available to be filled and poured out; or as a *servant* (v. 24) who is a love slave of the Lord God.

Does this sound like a tall order? Even impossible? Settle it at the start: being God's person—just like Jesus who was and did all that God designed Him to be and do—requires more than the raw materials we bring to the project. But that is why we need Jesus. Christ died for all our inadequacies and our weaknesses. What we must do is present ourselves as living sacrifices, holy (and wholly) to Him—it is only reasonable. We are not to settle down in our ordinariness, to be conformed to the mold of the apathetic world—even the world of Christians. We are to prove what is the good and perfect will of God (see Rom. 12:1-2).

This is a wonderful invitation to the world's greatest come-as-you-are party! Accept it, dress in the righteousness of Jesus Christ and present yourself. God will transform you into His servant—a servant-teacher, a servant-soldier, a servant-athlete, a servant-farmer, a servant-workman, a servant-vessel or a servant-leader. Be filled with His Spirit and watch Him change you!

I don't remember where I first heard this statement, but it has stayed with me, and I give it to you: *God loves you just the way you are—but too much to leave you that way!*

The one who serves you best will be your leader.

LUKE 22:25 TLB

Jesus

Give Me
Some Vitamin E!

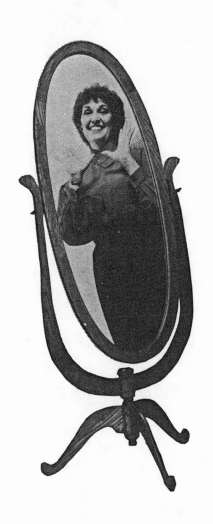

EQUIPPED FOR EXCELLENCE

When I turned the infamous or fabulous (depending on your point of view) 50 years of age a few years ago, several well-meaning friends had some advice for me.

Vitamin E would do wonders for this aging bod, I was told! I won't begin to tell you all the things they said it would do for me—nor will I reveal if it did! But perhaps the most important lesson learned in facing the potential prime time slump is this: I could use a good spiritual dose of vitamin E.

"When you turn 50 you have the face you deserve!" Winnie announced at my birthday party. Winnie is something like 16 months younger than me and is prone to remind me of this fact at strategic times. But vitamin E *is* supposed to keep your face from wrinkling. As I thought about Winnie's statement, I remembered lots of prime timers and postprime timers that I knew and the axiom seemed to be true.

Sharon has spent the last 50 years caring for others, serving her family, her Lord, her church and her community. The expression on her face, without the benefit of cosmetics, absolutely radiates the joy of the Lord. She has the face she deserves.

However, Dolores (her name was changed to protect the guilty!) has struggled through her life waiting to be "done for." Unfortunately, her attitudes have not only produced a permanent frown, but she has frequently been "done in."

On a rerun of "Little House on the Prairie," Mrs. Olsen was being given a beauty treatment by a traveling cosmetic saleslady.

"This cream will help to correct and hide those crow's feet around your eyes."

Indignantly, Mrs. Olsen retorted, "Those are not crow's feet! They are laugh lines!"

"Nothing could be that funny!" giggled the beautician.

Try as we will, our faces reveal our intake of vitamin E, both physically and spiritually.

Does your servant-leadership need a fresh dose of vitamin E?

Give Me an E for Energy!

Did you know that energy produces energy—like exercise? When we use our spiritual energy, as with our spiritual gifts, we are not exhausted but exhilarated and energized. When I am willing to use my abilities carefully and efficiently, I see God do what He promises to do in Philippians 2:13 *(AMP)*:

> [Not in your own strength] for it is God Who is all the while effectually at work in you—energizing and creating in you the power and desire—both to will and to work for His good pleasure and satisfaction and delight.

Give Me an E for Exceptional!

If you have read this far and are still open to taking another step in becoming what the Lord wants you to be, you are *exceptional*!

I am always amazed when anyone at all responds to a challenge to learn how to be a better servant! When I started teaching this course for women, and the tables would all be set up *exceptionally,* and the posters of these seven figures in 2 Timothy 2 would be in place, smiling on all who came through the door, my heart took a leap that anyone at all would come to hear or to learn! It isn't necessarily the most appealing idea in the world—the prospect of having more responsibility and more opportunity to keep "busy."

But we lay it right on the line at the outset: God will take you at your word! If you are willing to invest your time and apply yourself to excellence in serving, He will find you work!

It is certainly more comfortable to attend conferences and retreats to be inspired than to see yourself right there as the Master comes home to check on the stewardship of the servants to whom talents have been given. Do you remember what happened to those who had done well? Of course you do!

"You have been faithful with a few things; I will put you in charge of many things" (Matt. 25:21, *NIV.* See also verse 23). They didn't get a vacation, not on your life! They were given more work, more responsibility, and yet, greater reward.

It is something like the picture of the vessel in 2 Timothy 2:20-21. There are lots of very nice vessels in a household but there are only a few that are set apart for special service. They are vessels unto honor—no, one step further than that: they are *chosen* vessels, cleansed, exempted from ordinary uses, set apart for temple service. The Scripture teaches that we can *choose* to be chosen vessels, having been cleansed and being cleansed continually by applying 1 John 1:9 and becoming available to God's highest and holiest purposes. *Exceptional*—by choice!

Give Me an E for Expectation!

Let the *expectation* of the provision for your equipping be from Him. Someone has said that the ability or equipping follows the commitment. I think I believe that!

I also believe that we have a tendency to rise to what is expected of us.

Rollie was a typically difficult kid in our group of a dozen or so varied junior high kids in the church. Being the sponsor, I had dreamed up a talent program for a Sunday evening presentation. Not one of them was necessarily gifted, but most of the kids practiced at least an old piano recital piece or a magic trick, hoping for a revelation of spiritual truth in the sleight of hand. But Rollie just didn't have the gumption or grit to get his "talent" together.

I called him Sunday afternoon just to check. "What are you doing, Rollie?" I inquired. I heard a background whirring. Rollie answered, "I am making popovers."

"How about your talent for tonight's program? Have you decided what it is you want to do? We're counting on you!"

"Daisy, I don't have a talent."

"Rollie, bring all your stuff and show everybody how to make popovers! Be sure to bring some of your finished product because everyone will want a sample."

I guess I just wasn't prepared for Rollie. That night he moved into the church sanctuary—we had to use the sanctuary for the benefit of the pianists and organist in the group. Rollie set up his table, donned his chef's cap and stacked up the Tupperware bowls in order of use. Then he began, "Ladies and gentlemen, I am about to make popovers. I guess you could say it is a talent of mine. Actually, I didn't know it was my talent until Daisy called and told me so—."

What a compliment! Is it possible that God could use us in others' lives to call forth abilities and talents—equipping for service—that we don't even realize are there? Can we begin to *expect* that His Spirit within longs to respond to our *expectation* that He will give us what we need to "make the teaching about God our Savior attractive" (Titus 2:10, *NIV*)?

Emerson said, "Our chief want in life is someone to make us do what we can."

Kenneth Taylor, in *The Living Bible* has paraphrased three verses that fit right here: "O my soul, don't be discouraged. Don't be upset. *Expect* God to act!" (Ps. 42:11, italics added); "We confidently and joyfully look forward to actually becoming all that God has had in mind for us to be" (Rom. 5:2); "For I live in *eager expectation* and hope that I will never do anything that will cause me to be ashamed of myself but that I will always be ready to speak out boldly for Christ" (Phil. 1:20, italics added).

Give Me an E for Enthusiasm!

The root of enthusiasm is *en theos*—"in god." Let's claim this and be caught up in God-ness; having an attitude of being completely sold out, convinced and therefore convincing! This quality of being in God ought to be the hallmark of our life and service. Do not let familiarity or routine dull this most important quality in your leadership.

From a favorite book of mine:

Lord,
> it takes two hands to clap.
> It takes a total involvement—
> a caught-up-ness—
> to respond to thee.

Clapping is joy
> and response
> and approval
> and saying, "I'm with you.
> > Amen!"

And it takes two hands to clap.
One hand behind me, holding back, won't do it.

Clapping is enthusiasm.
> (Lord God, I cannot escape thee!
> Enthusiasm—*en theos*—possessed by God!)
> enthusiasm, with a little *e*,
> is a polite and brittle expression
> of a shallow sanction.

Enthusiasm—possessed by thee?
> Oh, may it be so!
> May there be no withholdings.
> Lord, possess my life.
> Take these, my hands—
> > both of them.
> > > Amen.[1]

"Serve the Lord enthusiastically" (Rom. 12:11, *TLB*).

Give Me an E for Example!

Without a doubt our most important tool for leadership is *example*. It is Jesus' idea! Jesus could have said, "Do as I say!" Instead, our Lord said, "Do as I do!" (see John 13:15). The apostle Paul says, "[Follow] my example" (Phil. 3:17, *NIV*).

Most of the listeners squirmed a bit when the leader suggested that each of us make a list of our own traits, habits or characteristics that we wish our children would emulate! Perhaps we understand the power of our *example* but it is uncomfortable to think too much about it. But how can we pray that the Lord will guard and keep our children—and others within our influence—pure and holy, and that He will protect them from the evil influences of this world—unless we are willing to set the example of holy living? Unless we are willing to say, "Do as I do!"

Have you heard about the young lady who was fixing her ham for Sunday dinner? Before she put the ham in the oven she cut off the end and threw it away, and then put the rest in the roasting pan. One of her guests observing her asked why she threw away that large piece.

"Well," she said, "I always saw my mother do it this way."

One day she had the opportunity and decided to ask her mother. Her mother then asked *her* mother why she had always thrown away the end of the ham.

"I don't know why *you* do it, but I had to because I never had a pan big enough!"

Is it time to check out your *example* to see how and what others follow?

This is a vitally important leadership principle. We must be willing to live so as to say, "Watch me, do as I do, and I will show you Christ's way. I am willing to be your example in service and in ministry." Philippians 3:17 says to follow my example. Can you accept this challenge to let the Spirit of God live His life through you so that you can, with a holy pride like Paul's, become a viable role model for your children, church or community?

Cathy Meeks, the assistant dean of women at Mercer University at Macon, Georgia, in her book *I Want Somebody to Know My Name*, writes of her childhood in a poverty-stricken home in the South. She came to Christ as a young girl and maintained her faith in spite of the extremely difficult circumstances in her home. Her childhood was scarred by the disdain for blacks in their community, her father's despair and hopelessness acted out in alcoholism, and her lack of guidance from a teacher or church. She says, "I remember searching throughout my teen years for a role model and I could not find one. As I grew up and became a college student in the '60s, my life and goals were changed when I decided to become a role model!"[2]

Example is our most potent leadership tool. But it involves great risk. The one "up front," the chairwoman, the leader, is the risk taker, becoming vulnerable to criticism and evaluation. When the speaker speaks, all the others—the listeners—can decide to accept or reject, make out a grocery list or take notes on the message—or even make a note to let the speaker know where she could get her hair done a bit more chicly. The saying: "To avoid criticism, do nothing, say nothing, be nothing" is true. But when the leadership opportunity arises, the challenge of the saying is inadequate to provide courage to do something, say something or be something.

But take heart, God will make of you a Proverbs 31 kind of woman and a 2 Timothy 2 kind of servant-leader if you let Him.

Give Me an E for Excellence!

In an article entitled, "Excellence: The Christian Standard," Senator Mark Hatfield wrote, "Our first responsibility is to utilize and mobilize the resources, the capacity, the intellect, the drive, the ambitions and all that God has given us, and to use them to the fullest. That comes first in whatever endeavor to which we are committed."[3]

Former Health, Education and Welfare Secretary John W. Gardner once said, "I am concerned with the fate of excellence in our society. If a society holds conflicting views about excellence, or cannot rouse itself to the pursuit of excellence, the consequence will be felt in everything it undertakes."[4]

Excellence in our service; let it be our goal. We can get by, even acceptably, with mediocrity: "Let's not go to any trouble this time! Let's keep it really simple." Simplicity itself is desirable, for complications occur without encouragement. But simplicity because of laziness is not a worthy goal. Remember that God's standard is *excellence*—perfection. His plan is for you to be conformed to the *excellence* of Jesus Christ. And in Him there is nothing mediocre.

Paul was in pursuit of *excellence*. If ever there was anyone who could have sat back resting on his qualifications and who did not get ruffled even after his encounter with the living God, it was Paul. Philippians 3 is a chronicle of his quest for excellence: "But whatever was to my profit I now consider loss for the sake of Christ. What is more, I consider everything a loss compared to the surpassing greatness of knowing Christ Jesus my Lord, for whose sake I have lost all things. I consider them rubbish, that I may gain Christ" (vv. 7-8, *NIV*).

Philippians 3 is Paul's priority chapter in his pursuit of *excellence*. The first step in his pursuit was to have a personal knowledge of Christ (see vv. 7,10). That is number one—the goal!

Second, his motivation (vv. 10-12) was that he aspired to actually become like Christ. That possibility became the motivation for all he did.

Third, he aggressively pursued *excellence*: "Forgetting what is behind and straining toward what is ahead, I press on toward the goal" (vv. 13-14, *NIV*).

Leroy Eims, in his book *Be the Leader You Were Meant to Be*, says that God works in our lives in at least seven ways to bring about a spirit of *excellence*:

1. By helping us realize our own weakness—2 Corinthians 12:9;
2. Through the prayers of others—Colossians 4:12;
3. Through someone sharing the Word with us—1 Thessalonians 3:10;
4. As we study the Bible for ourselves—2 Timothy 3:16-17;
5. Through suffering—1 Peter 5:10;
6. By giving us a hunger for holiness—2 Corinthians 7:1;
7. Through a desire to have the fruit of our lives brought to perfection—Luke 8:15.

"Some words of caution need to be sounded at this point. First, we need to examine our motivation. Excellence for its own sake is not our standard, but excellence for Christ's sake."[5]

School was fun for me—especially grammar school. Report card time held not much threat for me. But in spite of how well I did in grades, my dad's reaction was always the same: That and better will do! It would run through my head because Dad said it often—not just for report cards. He challenged his five daughters with a word of acceptance first, then a challenge to do better. I have been told that William Booth, the founder of the Salvation Army, inspired and challenged his "disciples" with those words and Dad just picked up on the theme. But it worked! Daddy built strongly on the foundation of acceptance—but no status quo sufficed for long.

A couplet comes to mind and I don't even remember where I first heard it:

Good, better, best,
never let it rest
Until your good is better
and your better-BEST!

Look, You're a Teacher!

THE GLORIFYING SERVANT-TEACHER

> "For you must teach others those things you and many others have heard me speak about. Teach these great truths to trustworthy [women] who will, in turn, pass them on to others" (2 Tim. 2:2, *TLB*).

To be an authentic Christian means that you will reveal the character of God through your life. That is what it means to glorify God—to show His character qualities through your lifestyle.

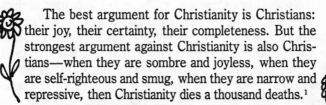

The best argument for Christianity is Christians: their joy, their certainty, their completeness. But the strongest argument against Christianity is also Christians—when they are sombre and joyless, when they are self-righteous and smug, when they are narrow and repressive, then Christianity dies a thousand deaths.[1]

Whether we like it or not, we are all teachers. The choice is ours as to what we teach. When I remember those who have been my teachers I often find it difficult to put my finger on exactly what I learned because the person who was my teacher spoke so much louder than did his or her words.

Meet My Teachers

I had a junior high teacher like that. She made us *want* to come to school! She always looked so nice. As I think of it now, there was nothing unusual about her clothes or her hairdo, but I do have a clear image that she was so well-groomed.

She had a kind of dignity about her that seemed to let us know that she was in charge and knew exactly what she would do next. Fred was always a problem to her, but she patiently accepted his homework and was determined to help Fred catch up so he could be promoted.

Miss DeVincenzo was the recipient of valentines and apples, notes and wildflowers—how we looked for ways to please her! She was a teacher who made us want to learn because she made it seem so very important just by being who she was.

Edith Schaeffer says in her book, *What Is a Family?* that home is the place where truth is transmitted—or ought to be. We are teachers in our own homes, transmitting the truth of the gospel in authentic living from one generation to another.

In the first chapter of 2 Timothy and again in Acts 16, we get a glimpse into Timothy's home. Imagine Paul knocking on the door of that little home and inquiring within, "Is there someone here who's been made ready and has been taught to serve the Lord?" Grandma Lois and Mother Eunice smile and say, "Here he is! A graduate of the school of homemade Christian education! Timothy is ready to go with you!"

I believe I have a knack with kids, or at least I used to think so. We were fresh and green to the staff of a children's home in northern California. One of my choicest assignments was to create a Sunday evening worship service for the kids from 7 to 11 years old. This unwieldy group of about 50 met in a room we liked to call the library. These were kids from all sorts of backgrounds—foster homes and juvenile halls—mostly wards of the court in the many counties of California. Every Sunday evening I would enlist a pianist from the staff and we would have a go at it. A good share of the kids had never been to Sunday School, much less to Sunday evening services. But dressed in the whole armor of God, we went to the fray.

I remember that this particular evening I was teaching the children about prayer. "Now we're going to pray," I said. But in order to involve them I suggested that maybe they could give us some prayer requests, some special things they thought we ought to pray about.

Many hands shot up and I called on them one at a time and we made our list:

"Margie's foster mother lost a check"; "Jim was really missing his dog"; "Felix had all his week's allowance stolen" and on and on we went.

When I finally had to call a halt to all we were about to take to the Lord I asked, while the piano was being played softly, if we could bow our heads and spend just a moment in silent prayer. I smiled. In my own "super-spiritual" way I was actually encouraging this amazing collection of kids in the fine art of prayer. I had my eyes closed, savoring the silence reverently. Yet inside I had this awful desire to peek. Finally that desire got the best of me and, with one eye open, I saw Darryl way in the back raise his hand.

I knew he was going to say something which was sure to contribute to the sweet spirit in that place so I inquired as to what it was he wanted. From the back of the room he yelled, "Hey, Daisy, you're all open in front." Sometimes even our best efforts seem to be thwarted. I buttoned my blouse and carried on.

Then there was Bobby, just eight years old. Bobby came to church every Sunday night waiting for the opportunity to share his Scripture verse. I would say, "Well, kids, remember we are all learning our verses. Isn't there someone here who has a special verse you have learned this week?"

Actually it was surprising that I even expected any of the kids to stop their fussing and feuding and eating and running and reading long enough to learn a Scripture verse, but Bobby raised his hand every Sunday night.

"Yes, Bobby, let's hear from you."

"Jesus said, don't say, 'shut up' to the cottage mother."

"Well, Bobby, that's certainly a good and important thought, but I don't think it's right from the Bible."

"Jesus said, quit stealing your friend's allowance."

Little by little, I tried to feed in the fact that just to put "Jesus said" in front of a good thought did not make it the inerrant Word of God. Bobby tried so hard to do what I find myself trying to do—add authority to my life by claiming all my behavior is guided by the Lord Jesus. Not too bad an idea after all, is it?

She Teaches Truth by Example

If the qualification of the 2 Timothy 2 teacher is that she is a transmitter of truth, it will do us well, servant-teacher to consider what is being transmitted through our lives.

Miss Hamel was my Sunday School teacher when I was just a little girl. My sisters and I attended the Christian and Missionary Alliance Sunday School near Times Square in New York City. Our parents were in the Salvation Army and our dad directed a center for alcoholics in "hell's kitchen" not far from where the Alliance Church was located.

Miss Hamel was a maiden lady who had a desire to transmit truth to the four or five of us who sat under her tutelage. It was back in those old days when flannelgraph was just being introduced as the ultimate visual aid. But Miss Hamel hadn't gotten that message yet and she was confident that she could get the truth of the Word into our mind without any newfangled aids. And she did! We were assigned a certain number of verses each week and we competed, winning bookmarks, colored buttons and especially her approval as we memorized and memorized.

She knew the Word could be depended upon to produce fruit in our lives and that it was not necessary that we understood all that the Beatitudes meant before we learned them, or Psalm 1, or Psalm 100, or John 1, and on and on and on. Now that I think about it, most of the Scripture I know by heart I learned before I was 12 years old! And if I had waited until I understood it, I wouldn't have it now!

❀ Be a Transmitter of Truth!

Select a verse of Scripture, memorize it and then teach it to someone else. Do you do this on a regular basis with your children?

🌸 Teach Truth

What is the *truth* you are teaching by your life?

Look up the following verses and make some notes to yourself about *how* you are living and sharing these fundamental truths of your faith:

1. Jeremiah 33:3 _____

2. 1 Kings 8:56 _____

3. Ephesians 2:8-10 _____

4. James 5:16 _____

5. Ephesians 5:20 _____

Use a concordance to look up other Scriptures that represent some new truth that God is showing you. First personalize—then publicize!

She Teaches Truth by Encouragement

Be a teacher who encourages!

Dr. Clyde Narramore believes that it is the right of every child to receive some encouragement every day. One teacher, Miss Johnson, accepted the challenge to do just that for those students within her influence. She mimeographed the list of students in her class and each day, checked the name of a student when she took the opportunity to encourage him or her. One day one of her students, Vincent, had been incorrigible—nothing about his person or behavior allowed for encouragement! As the final bell rang, signaling that she wouldn't see the children until the next day, Miss Johnson remembered her commitment to encouragement. She took a deep breath, patted Vincent as he left the room and said, "Vincent, you certainly were vital today!"

🌸 Examining Encouragement

1. Can you make a list of those in your life who are looking to you daily as an example or model?
2. Do you need to put a check by each name as you affirm, encourage and pray for those special people?

The teacher is constantly visualizing the realities of the Word of God to her students. Therefore,

What the teacher *says* is important,
What she *does* is more important, but
What she *is* is most important!

She Teaches Truth in Titus 2 Style

A Titus 2 directive says that older women are to teach the younger women to be quiet and respectful in everything they do. They must not go around speaking evil of others, they must not be heavy drinkers, they should be teachers of goodness, instead. These older women must train the younger women to live quietly, love their husbands and their children, and be sensible and clean minded. They should be pure, keepers at home, good and obedient to their own husbands, so the Word of God will be not blasphemed.

There is a marvelous church in southern California that has a unique women's ministry. I asked the pastor of this growing church, known for its teaching ministry, what part the women played in its phenomenal growth. He said one of their most effective programs is called Keepers-at-Home. Several older women invite four or five younger women to their homes where they spend a morning or an afternoon learning canning, quilting, breadmaking or ways to have a family altar with active children.

Then once a quarter the younger women sponsor a luncheon at the church for the ladies who had been willing to teach. They all "dress up and have someplace to go!" explained the pastor.

It is refreshing to realize that there are churches, alive and growing, where the middle-aged and older women are challenged to teach the younger women in such creative ways. Is your church ready for a Keepers-at-Home ministry?

Malettor Cross is a strong, dignified black mother of 11 children from Detroit, Michigan. Her eyes glistened with enthusiasm and zeal as she shared with me the burden on her heart for black women.

"The need is overwhelming for gut-level Bible teaching. The Word of God has not been taught to the blacks enough to bring about changed lives. The black community has been exploited by its own people and others. That is not to say that God has not raised up some fine, well-educated black teachers and preachers. But there have been so many others who have taught the Word when it has benefited *them,* for their own support, and not for the benefit of the hearer."

Mrs. Cross was now into her element. This was the passion of her heart—to teach teachers! She was talking so fast and vibrantly, I had a hard time keeping up—

"Yes, Daisy, that is what it is all about! In our conferences where we are trying to get black women to teach other black women, we want to scratch where it itches. We want to teach women not only how to be Christians, but how to live as Christians.

"This is my excitement now. I have two classes, one to train children's teachers and one to train Bible class instructors. I have let all my ladies know that they are expected to go out and teach others. I tell them to activate 2 Timothy 2:2—to go and teach others."

Malettor went on to say that she feels the government has been careful in recent years to provide blacks with opportunities for higher education. But the thousands who are graduating from colleges and universities each year are schooled in humanistic philosophies. Her heart's cry is that the Church of Jesus Christ will soon catch up—women teaching other women and our young people in the principles of the changeless Word of God.

❀ Titus 2 Ministering

1. Do you think a Titus 2 ministry refers to physical age only or could it also refer to those who are spiritually younger?
2. Have you had the experience of "an older woman in the Lord" teaching and discipling you? Discuss.
3. List the qualifications for women in Titus 2 and take a personal character inventory.
4. Do you have a teachable spirit? Are you willing to bring your life into line with the Word of God in order to serve Him and to become a role model?
5. Is it possible to fulfill Titus 2:3-5 *and* be employed outside your home?
6. What are some influences on your life that make it more difficult to fulfill this Scripture? What are some influences that encourage godliness?

She Teaches Truth with the Sweet Fragrance of Christ

My first-grade nephew Frankie told his mom, as she was getting him ready for school, to put his shoes on the wrong feet. "Whatever for?" she asked, as he kicked off his oxfords to the floor.

"Because—when I get to school my teacher will say, 'Frankie, you have your shoes on the wrong feet again!' and then she will sit me down and fix them—and Mom, I like the way she smells!"

But thanks be to God! For through what Christ has done, he has triumphed over us so that now wherever we go he uses us to tell others about the Lord and to spread the Gospel like a sweet perfume. As far as God is concerned there is a sweet, wholesome fragrance in our lives. It is the fragrance of Christ within us, an aroma to both the saved and the unsaved all around us (2 Cor. 2:14-15, *TLB*).

Noah built an altar and it says in the Word that "God smelled a sweet savor of his burnt offering. It was a sacrifice of praise, faith and thanksgiving.

Our lives can be that—a sweet smelling fragrance to the Lord. It is borne through a life of sacrifice.

Is that the air freshener in your home?

 How to Make a Pot Pourri Sachet

Materials: 4-inch embroidery hoops
2-5½-inch (or larger) pieces lacy fabric; a curtain remnant will do
¼ cup *pot pourri,* vitalized by rose oil or some other sweet-smelling oil
12 inches eyelet trim
15 inches contrasting ¼-inch width velvet ribbon

On the small ring of embroidery hoop lay one piece of fabric. Pour *pot pourri* onto center of fabric, laying second fabric piece on top. Seal with larger ring of embroidery hoop. Trim raw edge of fabric to underside of ring. With glue, place eyelet onto back of ring to form ruffled frame. Allow to dry for a few minutes. Then apply glue to outside of ring and cover with velvet ribbon. Make a bow from the extra ribbon and glue to front of frame. VOILA!

Therefore be imitators
of God—copy Him and follow
His example—as well-beloved
children [imitate their father].
And walk in love—esteeming and
delighting in one another—as
Christ loved us and gave Himself
up for us, a . . . sacrifice to God
[for you, so that it became]
a sweet fragrance.
Ephesians 5:1-2,
AMP.

EFFECTIVE TEACHING METHODS

Let's consider some of the teaching methods Jesus used.
You'll discover joy and success with your students.

Visual Tools

In John 8, Jesus was outside the Temple and a group of leaders and Pharisees put an adulteress on display in ridicule.
"'Teacher,' they said to Jesus, 'this woman was caught in the
very act of adultery. Moses' law says to kill her. What about it?'"
(John 8:4, *TLB*).

Silently, yet most eloquently, Jesus stooped and wrote in the
sand. How our imaginations have wondered what He wrote!
Whatever it was, there was a reaction, then pressure to verbal-
ize His answer so that they could criticize.

"Go ahead and throw stones at her—but let the one who is
without sin cast the first stone!" (see v. 7).

The Jewish leaders and others in the crowd left one by one
as Jesus stooped again and wrote silently. It is apparent that
whatever He wrote packed the punch necessary to convict and
disperse the crowd.

Barbara Johnson is the mother of a homosexual and her

book, *Where Does a Mother Go to Resign?* is priceless. She has a wit and humor that is a unique gift and a useful teaching tool. I'd love to share a quote from her book: "I'm always in the midst of an energy crisis and an identity crisis at the same time. I don't know who I am, but I am too tired to find out!"[2] Can we relate?

Anyway, she gave me a stone one day last fall. On it are painted some flowers and the words: Daisy's first stone. As she presented it to me she said, "Daisy, you must hang onto this. Actually, you might try to throw it some time, but you will probably never be able to follow through. It is a reminder of Jesus' words—that only those who are without sin can throw the first stone. Those of us who carry a first stone have grown to realize that none of us is perfect yet—and we just have to use our stones as paper weights or as kitchen windowsill reminders."

What a visual tool for combating the spirit of criticism!

 The First Stone

1. Find a smooth stone about three inches in diameter.
2. Wash and dry.
3. Paint a bright background on top of stone and decorate with flowers, etc.
4. Write with black felt-tipped marker, when the paint is

dry: _____ First Stone.
　　　　　　　　(your name)
5. Write John 8:7 on the back as a reminder!

Meet Your Audience on Their Territory

In Matthew 22:15-22 Jesus spoke again to the religious leaders. This time they tried to trap Him and trick Him into a conversation concerning the duty of a taxpayer. Jesus met them on their ground and asked them to show Him a coin—right out of their own pocket. A teaching tool and a principle of communication: meet your audience on their territory. Do not speak to a group of financiers on agriculture or to a group of single women on child rearing.

A Purse Full of Lessons

Take a few minutes to find an article in your own purse that you can use as an object lesson for your group.

Example: Your driver's license
Lesson: God knows who you are! See Isaiah 43:1.

Example: Your mirror
Lesson: We need to reflect the glory of the Lord! See 2 Corinthians 3:18.

Discussion

In John 4 Jesus met the woman of Samaria at Sychar's Well. The conversation was like a seesaw. The lady changed the subject just as often as she could and Jesus skillfully kept up with her. The topics ranged from racial prejudice to the history of Israel and from her marital status to places of worship. Each time Jesus came closer to accomplishing His purposes in the encounter. He used discussion—and so can you by being a good listener, asking questions at the appropriate times and extending a caring attitude that says, "I care about your feelings and your thoughts."

A Table Discussion

Let someone in your group briefly share her testimony or discuss the variety of ways God brought you to Himself.

Demonstration

In John 13, Jesus was in the Upper Room with His disciples and He illustrated how they were to serve. He could have simply told them but instead He filled a basin with water and, with a towel, knelt down in front of each man and washed his feet. Do you think they ever forgot this lesson?

May each of us give the
    Gift of Christ Himself
Not merely in the words you say,
Not only in the thought confessed
    Is Christ expressed
For me, 'twas not the truth you taught
To you so clear to me so dim,
But when you came to me you brought
    A sense of Him.
And from your eyes He beckons me
And from your heart His light is shed
Till I lost sight of you and see
    the Christ instead.[3]

Field Trip

A trip to the Temple to observe a widow giving all she had in the offering served to illustrate and then confirm the spirit in which each of us is to give. Jesus could have lectured on stewardship and invited pledges; instead He used a field trip. He only needed to summarize His lesson for maximum effectiveness.

Projects

After teaching the disciples Jesus sent them out two-by-two to practice. He knew that students learn by doing and He sent them to see people, to listen to them, to share their experiences and to share the message of salvation.

A Friendly Visit

Before your next get-together, find a partner and visit at least one neighbor to share your love and a plate of cookies! Or have a neighborhood coffee party with a partner and enjoy the fellowship.

Drama

And what a drama was played out in the Temple as Jesus made a whip and drove out the money changers! Although this example is more closely related to being dramatic than Jesus using drama to teach, it is still worth noting. Drama is an excellent tool for the teacher. The actors involved invariably have a deeper understanding of the drama being played out, they loose shyness and *they* become teachers without realizing it. Forethought and planning are a must for the teacher who wishes to use drama as a teaching tool, but the rewards are exciting.⁴

Teach by Singing

The Lord teaches us truths meant to be sung in our lives. Look up the following verses and identify the circumstances and themes of these songs:

1. Psalm 149:3: _____

2. Psalm 119:54-55: _____

3. Exodus 15:1-2: _____

God has given us directives to teach others in song. Look up these verses and discover the content of these songs:

1. Deuteronomy 31:19, 21: _____

2. 1 Kings 4:32: _____

3. Ephesians 5:19: _____

4. Colossians 3:16: _____

Some day there is to be a song sung by all those whom the Lord has created in His image. Created creatures are to join in a magnificent song, outliving history and praising the living God in a choir that cannot be numbered.

Will we be there? Jesus, the Lamb of God, and Moses are to be there. And the song is a special blend of theirs: "And they sing the song of Moses the servant of God, and the song of the Lamb, saying, Great and marvelous are thy works, Lord God Almighty; just and true are thy ways, thou King of saints. Who shall not fear thee, O Lord, and glorify thy name? For thou art holy; for all nations shall come and worship before thee; for thy judgments are made manifest" (Rev. 15:3-4, *KJV*).

The song within us now is meant to be a beginning. The crescendo, as every other instrument joins in, will come later.[5]

TEACH OTHERS BY SPEAKING IN PUBLIC

Our daughter and I walked into the department store in the busy shopping mall, armed with our charge card and what we thought was an impenetrable sales resistance.

"Step right up, ladies, and let me show you what this knife is able to do for you! Come in closer, let's have no gaps in our audience . . . cuts through your frozen food like butter . . . slices for your salads in seconds . . . stainless, serrated, safe (safe??), sturdy . . . *plus* . . . a scraper if you buy right now." On and on with staccato rhythm—and *we fell for it!*

The same knife and satellite utensils had lain for weeks, perhaps, on the counter in the store. But get it into the hands of a master salesman—who also demonstrates—and it was like a shotgun sales pitch. A very successful one, I might add, as the knives and scrapers and graters hit their targets in the crowd, while the cash register and plastic puncher recorded the sales.

Is that what we need in the church? Is that enthusiasm needed in your life? Isn't that what *real* teaching is? A demonstration.

The early Christians found the secret and they weren't selling knives or hawking nonessentials. They were called to be demonstrators, not displays. Displays are static—without animation—dead.

Demonstrations are active—animated—alive! The Apostle Paul writes to the Corinthians and to us in words we can identify with:

In the same way, my brothers, when I came to proclaim to you God's secret purpose, I did not come equipped with any brilliance of speech or intellect . . . . As a matter of fact, in myself I was feeling far from strong; I was nervous and rather shaky. What I said and preached had none of the attractiveness of the clever mind, but it was a demonstration of the power of the Spirit of God! Plainly God's purpose was that your faith should rest not upon man's cleverness but upon the power of God (1 Cor. 2:1-5, *Phillips*).

Have you ever felt like Paul did when he wrote this letter? He knew he would never be a clever public speaker and actually that wasn't his goal—he simply wanted to be a demonstration of the power of God.

Do you fear speaking in front of a group?

Did you know that this is the second greatest fear of the American people? The first is nuclear holocaust and the second is to speak in front of a group. Consider adopting a 1 Corinthians 2 mindset and make your purpose for speaking—as well as behaving—simply to be a vital, active demonstration of the power of God. Face this fear by perfecting simple skills and you'll see God's purposes fulfilled as you are given opportunities to "teach" in this way.

After all, we have not been left here on earth to decorate the church, but to demonstrate His power in visible, credible, authentic living.

The ABCs of Public Speaking

The servant-teacher must be poised in front of a group. This is the leadership characteristic we will consider now.

So you are invited to make a speech, give a devotion or share your testimony. Well, you have several choices:

1. decline and leave town;
2. accept, play hookey and find a substitute to take your place;
3. accept and cram until your nerves are standing on end and your family considers going on strike;
4. order a film;
5. accept and carefully develop a lesson plan.

Assuming you have settled on option 5, sharpen your pencil and do your homework. Following are some basic ABCs.

Accept the challenge and presume upon the Lord's enabling to communicate through you. "I can do everything through him who gives me strength" (Phil. 4:13, *NIV*).

An awareness of time allotted will be appreciated by everyone.

Appropriateness in dress is key and if in doubt, ask. Wear something you have worn before and are comfortable in. Wear a color that flatters you and makes a bold statement. Do not wear chains or jewelry that will distract. A skirt is always appropriate, though pants and pantsuits are not always so. Wear a long skirt if you are comfortable in one. Be certain that your clothes are not too tight for you.

Now, I am a tall woman and enjoy wearing long skirts when I speak. (I think I feel that it is a good way to cover up runs in my stockings!) I always wear a daisy, too—usually a pin—but I have a navy blue sweater with embroidered daisies on it and it makes a statement! A yellow blouse with a long tie bow goes well under it and the bow looks good filling in the v-neck of the sweater.

No one in the room will ever forget a night service at a large Winning Women Retreat in Florida. I stepped to the pulpit and, after a few opening remarks, launched into the main part of the message. Then I led the women to a portion of Scripture. I leaned over and picked up my bifocals (the better to see the words with, my dear) and lifted the glasses to my waiting eyes and nose. Inadvertently (how else?) I brought the long yellow ends of the tie with them! I couldn't see! The tie was making a blindfold of my bifocals! When I realized that the lights had not gone out and that the trouble was with me and my glasses, I wanted to have the platform open up and swallow me. The ladies were by that time laughing uproariously—and it was *not* a humorous part of the message. What poise I produced under that incredible pressure! Pulling myself together, I didn't even refer to it but moved right along. None of us will ever forget it, however!

Be yourself. You are unique and no one will communicate just like you. Unique does not even take an adjective; you are not very unique or almost unique or less or more unique—you have a style and message all your own. Let the Lord use the you that you are.

Be prepared. Of course you will have all your thoughts in order, but take the time before the meeting begins to check the lectern and microphone. It is distracting and time-consuming to have to work with these arrangements during the gathering.

Be careful to eat lightly, if at all, before speaking. This one makes me chuckle a little because I guess I eat everything put in front of me, at any time, and mostly out of nervousness!

Confidently communicate. If you have prepared and prayed that the Lord would communicate His message through you— even if it is only an announcement or an introduction of another speaker—be confident that He will bless your efforts. Do your part in preparation and expect that God will do His. The most difficult part of your message is to leave the results with Him.

Cut out fillers—the ahs, ers, ums and others! Practicing with a tape recorder will reveal to you these weaknesses which you can correct with more practice.

Cultivate an audience rapport and make eye contact with two or three friendly faces right away. I can almost always pick out of an audience those who have been in front of a group before. Can you imagine how? You are right! They are the ones who are making eye contact with me, smiling their support and paying attention. Anyone who has been there, who has taken the risk to be "on display" by sharing their thoughts and information for consideration and evaluation, are your friends. Make eye contact with them.

Cards are good for notes. Don't use large sheets of paper or pages from a loose-leaf notebook.

Don't read your speech. All flexibility is lost and you often lose your audience if you resort to reading what you have carefully prepared.

Don't grasp the lectern. Stand tall and straight.

Exercise ahead of time by giving your speech in a mirror to yourself or to your family. They will probably give you helpful criticism.

Excuses or apologies are a no-no. Do not bore your audience with the reasons you are not prepared or doing better or unqualified or any problems relating to the meeting, etc. This is an unprofessional defense mechanism. Perhaps we hope to get the sympathy of the hearers; instead we launch our speech with a negative distraction and we reveal our inadequacy. They will notice it soon enough!

Enthusiasm in your voice inflections will enhance your speech. Listening to a tape of your speech will help you to know how you are doing.

It is good practice to prepare a three-minute speech of about 250 words. Your own testimony or a brief segment of your own story is a good place to begin. And remember it is far more difficult to say something with purpose and power in three minutes than it is to prepare a half hour or an hour's presentation. You must be very selective and you will do well to adhere to the four steps listed: Wake up! Why? Watch! and What next?

Wake Up!

Begin your talk by assuming that your audience is asleep and needs to be awakened. Don't count on the fact that they are waiting eagerly for what you are about to say. Imagine your listeners as bored—and about to register a loud ho-hum!

Why?

Be ready to build a bridge with your second thought. Convey right away that your listener is involved in some way with the message content. Why are you telling them? It is because their lives are affected in some way—and let them be able to identify the relevancy.

Watch!

This is a demand of the listener, the for instance, the show me! As the examples are stated, make sure they are presented in good order, and actually illustrate your points—interesting, humorous, personal, historical, biblical—the list can go on indefinitely. Make notes of stories, signs along the highway, or other resources for illustrations for your speeches.

What Next?

Now is the time to ask for specific action. Make it perfectly clear what action or response you expect from the audience. Stand! Join! Contribute! Buy! Write! Your closing statements must summarize and challenge and tie up loose ends.

Sponsor's Checklist

Let me share a homework checklist for sponsors—for the care and feeding of speakers. If you are responsible for contacting speakers and developing programs for your women's organization, learn to do it with grace.

1. Develop an acquaintance with potential speakers and their ministries.
2. Title a file folder "Resource People" and collect names, addresses, phone numbers and brochures of speakers.
3. When considering a speaker, it is helpful to listen to a tape or attend a meeting where the person is speaking.
4. When contacting the speaker, remember:
   a. state clearly the purpose of the gathering
   b. identify the group or church making the request

    c. state the time, place and date of the meeting

    d. discuss the honorarium—20¢ a mile is the "going rate" for automobile travel; air fares are complicated and it is perhaps a good idea to check on possible economy air travel before the speaker is contacted.

✔ 5. And—Here she is! Just introduce the speaker.

    a. Don't attempt a biography, just a few well-prepared sentences.

    b. Don't wait until the speaker arrives to find out about her. The hostess will be able to give you some details because of her contacts.

    c. A long introduction is as inappropriate as one that is too short: "I don't know much about Mrs. _____,

so we will let her tell us about herself."

Practice Makes Perfect

Here's an idea or two that might inspire you to launch into a speaking ministry of your own—or at least help you to conquer a phobia of speaking in front of a group.

1. Plan a book report using the listener's laws. Give it while seated in an easy chair, with a cup of coffee in your hand, as if talking to yourself in reflection.

2. Introduce a speaker as if you were the master of ceremonies on the "This Is Your Life" program.

3. Using a telephone for a prop, make an announcement for an upcoming event by sharing the particulars enthusiastically with an imaginary friend. Be sure to use your imagination and creativity!

4. Demonstrate a craft idea, having copied the directions for each of the women in attendance. "How-to's" are one of the most difficult kinds of presentations to make!

5. Before refreshments are served, give a three-minute story of how you found the recipe for the dessert. Then let everyone have a taste. Or perform a monolog about its preparation with you in apron and chef's hat.

6. Give your own testimony. Start with a verse of Scripture that is most significant to you in planning your three-min-

ute speech. But *please* do not begin by saying, "This verse is very special to me." Instead, *wake up* your listeners with a "grabber" from your own *you*-nique life experience!

The young minister was giving his first after-dinner speech before a large audience and he felt extremely nervous. Before long he gave up. "My dear friends," he told his listeners, "when I came here this evening only God and I knew what I planned to say to you. Now only God knows!"

Write your own:

POISED AND PREPARED

It has only happened twice but, as far as I am concerned, twice is too often! I had a morning appointment and felt rather proud that I was clever enough to work in two activities—the coffee appointment with a lady who needed a broad shoulder to lean on for an hour or so, and the spring luncheon planned by a Methodist church in a suburb. It was April in Minneapolis and I set out with spring in my step.

Excusing myself from the coffee meeting I hurried (by now I was running too close to the luncheon time) and parked in the Methodist church lot. Rushing in, I said to the lady at the entrance—the one I was sure had been sent out to wait for the tardy speaker—that I was Daisy Hepburn and gave her my regrets. She looked quizzically, but asked me to follow her. Hardly waiting for her, much less following her, I dashed up behind the speaker's table and presented myself—hopefully in time for the buffet line. The chairwoman swung around as she heard me, looked me square in the eye and said, "You're for May!" Without stopping for lunch—without stopping for *anything*—I got out of there.

When I had to have a rerun the next month, I just entered as coolly as if nothing had happened at all!

It is such a good idea to call the speaker a day or two ahead of time to make certain that calendars are, in fact, coordinated!

David and I have given up presenting programs for Sweetheart Banquets. Actually, we gave them up a few years ago and I think it was right after our experience with the Baptists at the Swiss Chalet Restaurant.

We arrived in plenty of time, with a car loaded with a guitar, slide projector (for an audiovisual musical presentation) and even a cardboard bicycle-built-for-two. We went into the banquet room where the employees were arranging and setting tables. David kind of snapped his fingers and got the attention of the young man moving the chairs. "Will you please move the piano over here and then find me an extension cord so that I can set up this projector, and, and . . . . " There seemed to be a hesitancy and we began to wonder if good help was available at all anymore.

The clock said 6:30 P.M. and there didn't seem to be a Baptist in sight! Finally I had the nerve to inquire, "Isn't this banquet set for 6:45? Where do you think the folks are with the flowers and programs?"

The waitress went back to the office and returned to say, "This is an office party and it is scheduled for 7:30. *The manager of Woolworth's* will be here at 7:00 to finalize the arrangements."

The date for the Baptist banquet was *February* 28 not *January* 28! This time, dressed to our teeth, we stayed for supper anyway. We were the most outstandingly attired but most thoroughly embarrassed pair eating that night!

Be a servant-teacher who is poised and prepared to speak. And enjoy it! God has an abundance of blessings in store for you.

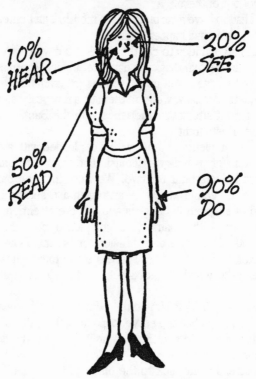

Take along some props to hold audience attention...

❀ An Arithmetic Problem

Number of days God created before He rested. _____

Plus, the number of days it rained on the Ark. **+** _____

Minus, the number of kinds of soil in Jesus' Parable in Matthew 13. **−** _____

Divided by the number of thieves who hung by Jesus on the cross. **÷** _____

Multiplied by the number of Noah's sons. **✕** _____

Divided by the number of people who lived in Martha's Bethany home. **÷** _____

Minus the number of loaves in the little boy's lunch. **−** _____

The Answer is the number of Jacob's sons. **=** _____

✻ Bible Books Puzzle

In these remarks are hidden the names of fifteen books of the Bible. It's a real lulu. Kept me looking so hard for the facts, I missed the revelation. I was in a jam especially since the names were not capitalized. The truth will come to many numbers of our readers. To others it will be a real job. For all, it will be a most fascinating search. Yes, there will be some easy to spot and some hard for the judges. So we admit it usually results in loud lamentations. One lady says she brews coffee while she puzzles over it.

1. _____   6. _____   11. _____

2. _____   7. _____   12. _____

3. _____   8. _____   13. _____

4. _____   9. _____   14. _____

5. _____   10. _____   15. _____

✿ Bible Book Mix-Up

Mrs. Thompson's Sunday School class was planning to make a poster showing what they had learned last month. Somebody dropped the sets of letters and now they're all mixed up. The students have neatly laid out the letters in groups of two, as all the books they learned are all composed of six letters. Can you discover which books they are by taking two letters from each of the three columns? An example has been underlined and entered for you.

1.	<u>EX</u>	AL	EL	_____
2.	JO	MU	AH	_____
3.	JU	<u>OD</u>	ER	_____
4.	SA	NI	MS	_____
5.	ES	AI	UA	_____
6.	PS	SH	<u>US</u>	_____
7.	IS	DG	EL	_____
8.	DA	TH	ES	_____

Psalm 106:1, KJV, Word Search

```
B F O N W Y X I F B Y A F G L F E D A
C H G M V E Z H G C Z X C O A G S C B
D K J L V P R J E S I A R P B K H I J
N M L I K Q S N K L M D R S N T S K L
F F G J I T D F X Z N O W A V U Q M N
C O A H U U N T O A P Q H L Q R S O P
E B R G R V W C B F L T S M 1 0 6 : 1 R
O H P E F Y X T G K O H E T P M N B A
R Q T E V Z H E F J I R U V P H E C D
S H C D A E C D V X C X H W O G F I J
U T I H L B R H W Y R Y Z I N M L K U
V W J O B D I J P T S A B J S Q R S T
X Y R A O C K L T U Z A C I I V W X J
Z D K O E F M N S V Y B E G H G C D H
A B G L F P O Q R W X H D E F F E B B
```

PRAISE	FOR
YE	HE IS
THE	GOOD:
LORD.	FOR HIS
O GIVE	MERCY
THANKS	ENDURETH
UNTO	THE LORD;

Instructions: The hidden words listed above appear in the puzzle forward, backward, up, down and diagonally. Find each word and put a box around it as shown in the example.

❀ My Prayer

Teach me, Lord, to keep sweet and gentle in all the events of life, in disappointments, in thoughtlessness of others, in the insincerity of those I trusted, in the unfaithfulness of those on whom I relied.

Help me to put myself aside, to think of the happiness of others, to hide my little pains and heartaches, so that I may be the only one to suffer from them.

Teach me to profit by the suffering that comes to me. Help me to use it that it may mellow me, not harden or embitter me; that it may make me broad in my forgiveness; kindly, sympathetic, and helpful.[6]

Look, You're a Soldier!

BACK TO THE BASICS

Take your share of suffering as a good soldier of Jesus Christ . . . and as Christ's soldier do not let yourself become tied up in worldly affairs, for then you cannot satisfy the one who has enlisted you in his army (2 Tim. 2:3-4, *TLB*).

Another go-around at basic training seems to be what we really need. A refresher course of following the leader into the basic essentials in soldiering, as found in Scripture.

When analyzing my Christian soldiering I discover the role of homefront recruiter to be comfortable and certainly more appealing than flapping about in boots and helmet in the infantry. As a matter of fact, I can imagine my continual opting for furloughs and "R and R's," not necessarily wanting a discharge but neither wanting the risk of being wounded!

Join the Distinctive Ranks

Christ's soldier is committed to the Commander and not to the affairs of the world. The soldier is single-minded, willing to stand in obedience and to forego many good things in order to please the Commander, the One who has chosen him to be a soldier.

In your ministry do you find it difficult to identify with the commitments of the soldier? "Worldliness" is almost an outmoded word. My dad used to say to us, when we dared to put on a little lipstick or even earrings, "Oh my, girls, you look too worldly!" Both by demand and desire I wanted to please my dad and it took some time before I even asked his permission to wear lipstick. The price of his disapproval was too high to pay.

Set-apartness, separation from the world—a distinctiveness about those in the service of the Lord—is harder to find now than it used to be. The enemy of our souls, our homes and our families—even our nation—is not asleep. We will be a more effective "army" if we are willing to be identified, both in attitude and action, as women who are effective because we are loyal to the Commander of the universe.

One day, while thinking about the necessity of setting ourselves apart from the world, I ran across an old article that I trust will clarify this "order" even further. (And may I suggest that you read it while listening to "Onward, Christian Soliders"!)

> Last Sunday our pastor asked Jimmy Mitchell, just back from two years at the front lines, if he'd be guest speaker at our church. Jimmy refused at first. Then with a funny light in his eye, he asked if the congregation would sing, "Onward, Christian Soldiers" just before he began. So we gave forth with the song and Jimmy waded in. This is what he said:
>
> "You have been singing, 'Like a mighty army moves the church of God.' That might have been all right once. The trouble now is that about ten million men know exactly how an army moves and it doesn't move the way a lot of you folks in our church do. Suppose the army accepted the lame excuses that many of you think are good enough to serve as alibis for not attending church.
>
> "Imagine this, if you can. Reveille 7 A.M. Squads on the parade ground. This sergeant barks out, 'Count fours. One! Two! Three! Number four missing. Where's Private Smith?'
>
> "'Oh,' pipes up a chap by the vacant place. 'Smith was out late last night and needed the sleep. He said he would be with you in spirit.'
>
> "'That's fine,' says the sergeant. 'Remember me to him! Where's Brown?'

"'Oh,' put in another chap, 'he's playing golf. He gets only one day a week for recreation, you know.'

"'Sure, sure,' the sergeant cheerfully answers. 'Hope he has a good game. Where's Robinson?'

"'Robinson,' explains a buddy, 'is sorry not to greet you in person, but he is entertaining guests today. Besides, he was at drill last week.'

"'Thank you,' says the sergeant, smiling. 'Tell him he's welcome any time he is able to drop in.'

"Did any conversation like that ever happen in the army? Don't make me laugh. Yet you hear stuff like that every week in the church, and said with a straight face, too.

"'Like a Mighty Army!' If our church really moved like a mighty army, a lot of you folks would be court-martialed!"[1]

> Like a mighty army
> Moves the Church of God;
> Brothers (and sisters), we are treading
> where the saints have trod;
> We are not divided, all one body we;
> One in hope and doctrine, one
> in charity![2]

As the strains of the martial music die out, it is my hope that these words will linger and serve to challenge us as soldiers in the Lord's army.

Loyalty

> Who is on the Lord's side?
> Who will serve the King?
> Who will be His helpers,
> Other lives to bring?
> Who will leave the world's side?
> Who will face the foe?
> Who is on the Lord's side?
> Who for Him will go?[3]

Think back for a moment to Esther, the Jewish queen of Media-Persia during the reign of King Ahasuerus. Even though she had spent at least 10 years living in security, luxury and in a position of prestige when trouble first began, she was willing to risk it all because of her loyalty to God and His chosen people. With a death sentence hanging over the heads of the Jews and realizing that she was the only one imminently qualified to refute the works of the Satan-like Haman, Esther picked up the gauntlet and fought. How easily she could have shut out the cries of those outside the palace walls who were unable to fight for themselves. Retreating to her own quarters would have been so much easier after all. But Esther chose the way of the soldier as we see in Esther 7:3-4,6 *(TLB):*

> "Your Majesty, save my life and the lives of my people. For I and my people have been sold to those who will destroy us. We are doomed to destruction and slaughter . . . . This wicked Haman is our enemy."

Let us declare ourselves to be *for* all that God is *for* and *against* all that God is *against*! We must have the courage to identify and face the enemy of our souls, our families and our churches. Then, at the risk of our personal comfort (ouch!) and security (ouch!), declare our identification with the Captain of our salvation and stand against sin.

> Stand up, stand up for Jesus,
> Stand in His strength alone;
> The arm of flesh will fail you,
> Ye dare not trust your own;
> Put on the gospel armor,
> Each piece put on with prayer,
> Where duty calls or danger,
> Be never wanting there.[4]

❀ A Lesson on Loyalty

Esther realized she had been _____. Have
Esther 2:17
you? See 1 Peter 2:9.

Esther realized she had been _____ for
Esther 4:14
special work. Have you? Now read 2 Timothy 3:15-17 in *The Living Bible*.

- How has God been preparing you for His service?
- Can you identify some pressure points in your life that call forth loyalty to Jesus Christ and His cause?
- Are you identifiable as a Christian in your community?
- When the enemy of your soul rears his ugly head, do you find yourself rising to the occasion in loyal defense of your faith?

Be Prepared

Have you ever heard of a "spiritual streaker"? This individual wears the helmet of salvation but none of the other necessary pieces of armor! Downright foolish is this Christian who makes an attempt to stand for Christ without benefiting from the protection and power obtained from the equipment listed in Ephesians 6.

The Belt of Truth (see Eph. 6:14). This belt or girdle covers the body, giving strength and support. The truth of the Word of God in our minds and in our hearts (see Josh. 1:8) will deal with our problem of confusion.

The Breastplate of Righteousness (see Eph. 6:14). The covering for our hearts, from which flow all the issues of life, is to be His righteousness. Claiming His forgiveness for our self-righteousness is part of our preparation and helps us deal with our problem of guilt.

Shoes of Peace and Witness (see Eph. 6:15). As children we sang, "Be careful little feet where you go, there's a Father up above, and He's looking down in love, oh, be careful little feet where you go!" These shoes signify a daily desire to walk His paths and yet another preparation to share Jesus Christ with others. Can these shoes deal with our problems that stem from a lack of purpose?

The Shield of Faith (see Eph. 6:16). Can you picture warriors of long ago going into battle with their large shields, often larger than the soldier himself? As the enemy approached, the shields were lined up in front of the soldiers to form a wall of protection against that first awful onslaught of arrows. Perhaps we need to produce our shields and line up with other soldiers, forming a first line of defense against temptation. The shield of faith can deal with this problem of temptation. "Without faith it is impossible to please *and* be satisfactory to Him" (Heb. 11:6, *AMP*).

The Helmet of Salvation (see Eph. 6:17). Let our thoughts be brought under His captivity and our minds be assured that what Jesus Christ won for you and me at Calvary—our salvation—is our possession! Let this assurance deal with our problem of doubt.

The Sword of the Spirit—which is the Word of God (see Eph. 6:17). This is our weapon, the only part of the armor that is for offense. The application of the Word of God to our conscience will deal with our attitude problem. Following Jesus' example (see Matt. 4) we can fight off Satan by the proper application of Scripture itself.

Prayer—the ultimate weapon. Ephesians 6:18 *(AMP)* helps us with these words: "Pray at all times—on every occasion, in every season—in the Spirit, with all (manner of) prayer and entreaty. To that end keep alert and watch with strong purpose *and* perseverance, interceding in behalf of all the saints (God's consecrated people)." Is our lack of victory related directly to our carelessness in prayer? Let this weapon deal with our problem of powerlessness!

❀ Spiritual Armor

Since we can only fight God's battles with spiritual weapons and never secular ones, discover how Jesus equipped His followers, according to the following Scriptures:

1. John 13:1 _____

2. Matthew 5:2 _____

3. Luke 22:39 _____
4. Matthew 10:5
   Luke 10:1 _____

❀ Strange Weapons?

Look up the battle accounts in Scripture and note the weapons used in each:

	Weapons
1. Exodus 7-11	_____
2. Joshua 6:16	_____
3. Judges 15:15	_____
4. Judges 7:20	_____
5. 1 Samuel 17:50	_____
6. 2 Chronicles 20:22	_____

Can you see how God uses ordinary things to gain the victory? What is God asking you to use to gain spiritual victories in your life and in the lives of those around you?

Are you a musician? How might God use your piano or your voice?

Are you a secretary? Can a typewriter be a weapon for God? How about your telephone? What is that in your hand?

Be Obedient

> True-hearted, whole-hearted, faithful and loyal,
> King of our lives, by Thy grace we will be;
> Under the standard exalted and royal,
> Strong in Thy strength we will battle for Thee.
> True-hearted, whole-hearted, fullest allegiance
> Yielding henceforth to our glorious King;
> Valiant endeavor and loving obedience
> Freely and joyously now we would bring. [5]

Obedience is one thing but loving, free and joyous obedience is something else! "True-hearted, whole-hearted, faithful and loyal," we sing. It is easier to sing it than to do it, don't you think? Remember how the Israelites greeted Moses' news that God had given him some laws for them to obey? "If God says we have to obey them, then we certainly will!" (see Exod. 19:8).

Submission to authority is basic to Christian soldiering. And the Israelites found out that they were not all that successful in their "whole-hearted obedience." Submission to anything or anyone is definitely out of style in this permissive society of ours. But submission to one another and submission to the laws and principles of our God is the standard of Scripture.

Barbara is an enthusiastic pastor's wife and retreat leader in Texas. In less than 10 years, the retreat ministry from their Baptist church has grown to attract over 1,000 women in two sessions. When someone inquired about her format Barbara's answer reflected definite and simple goals. There are always seminars offered in addition to the general sessions. All retreat first-timers have their seminars scheduled and there are three topics each considers: spirit-controlled living, the act of marriage and submission to authority.

Dear soldier in servant-leadership, we not only need to be reminded and often retrained to submit to authority in our lives, but we need to know how to teach this scriptural attitude to our children. I have a little story that says it best.

Three-year-old Bobby stood up in the front seat of the car while his mother backed out of the parking space. "Sit down,

Bobby!" instructed his mother as she glanced in her rearview mirror. After seeing no response from her normally cooperative son, she demanded again, "Sit down or I'll have to sit you down!" Reluctantly Bobby submitted to the tug on his size four jeans and sat down. A minute or two later, as she started out of the parking lot, she heard a small defiant voice mutter, "I'm standing up inside!"

Lots of times during my service to the Lord I have felt like I was obeying but standing up inside. At those moments I have learned to depend on Philippians 2:12 and 13 and I think it has become the most important part of my soldiering equipment. Let me quote them for you from *The Amplified Bible:*

> Therefore, my dear ones, as you have always obeyed [my suggestions], so now, not only [with the enthusiasm you would show] in my presence but much more because I am absent, work out . . . your own salvation . . . [not in your own strength] for it is God Who is all the while effectually at work in you—energizing and creating in you the power and desire—both to will and to work for His good pleasure *and* satisfaction *and* delight.

After looking at my calendar I nearly fainted! I saw another one of those meetings at which I was scheduled to speak . . . and tonight of all nights! I was exhausted and couldn't understand how I had missed that note on the calendar until now. I realized that it was a small church, a 25-mile distance from home, and I would probably be speaking without an honorarium.

As I prepared supper for my family, it was a struggle to get my mind and heart prepared for the evening's responsibility. Along the way, I prayed aloud—as I often do when I'm alone in the sanctuary of my Chevette—and a small miracle occurred. The Lord gave me the *want to*—the will and the desire to obey Him! As I ponder it now it is not all that small of a miracle. Claim it as a part of your equipment, for God has promised to give you the desire to obey. It's time to presume upon that promise so you can obey with gladness.

It was a grand evening at that little church and the Lord

blessed us all, especially me, with the exhilaration of being in the right place at the right time—obediently. I left humbly, clutching the gift of three cakes of perfumed soap as my honorarium. It may not have put gas in our tank but the Lord received the victory in another skirmish with myself!

❈ Battle Strategy: Obedience!

Turn to 2 Chronicles 20 and read about the attempted invasion of Judah. Now summarize in one sentence the battle strategy:

1. Preparation for battle: _____

_____

_____ (2 Chron. 20:4-14)

2. Strategy for battle: _____

_____

_____ (2 Chron. 20:15-20)

3. Weapons for battle: _____

_____

_____ (2 Chron. 20:21-23)

4. Outcome of battle: _____

_____

_____ (2 Chron. 20:24-30)

There is not much call for generals in Scripture, for God makes those selections. But as a soldier you can volunteer

to follow, and being so convinced of the cause, your life and attitude will quite naturally recruit others.

One day, while planning for a senior high week at Bible camp,
I got the idea to supply our eager campers with a good stiff lesson involving basic training for the Lord's Army.

"Yes, Mrs. Hepburn, I do have a few minutes available. Why
don't you come on over to Camp Ripley this morning?" As I hung
up the phone, I squealed in delight. The colonel, the ranking offi-
cer at one of the Midwest's largest National Guard encamp-
ments, had listened to my idea and certainly sounded ready to
cooperate. Maybe he hadn't heard me correctly but I ran to the
car and decided to find out face-to-face.

"Colonel, we have about 150 high school young people coming to camp next week and we need some 'local color' to add to
their understanding of the Lord's Army." About that time I was
sure he was thinking of lending me a parachute or a mess kit for
an object lesson. But I had far more than that in mind.

"Is there a possibility of your sending over a tank or two, or
a platoon of National Guardsmen, or maybe—." As the colonel's
eyes widened he pushed his chair back from the desk and took a
pencil in hand. Surprise of all surprises, he made some notes,
then picked up the telephone. Summoning one of his aides he
gave instructions to do "something for Mrs. Hepburn."

That something turned out to be five National Guard vehi-
cles driving down 23 miles of dirt road to be a part of the opening
night of camp! The National Guardsmen took our inductees for
rides on the amphibian, the jeep, the derrick and the half-ton
truck. They also played a wild game of softball with our
campers. I nearly invited them to stay for supper in the mess
hall but it was clear they were enjoying the girls a bit too much!

On Thursday morning, after a middle-of-the-night air raid
drill and dawn calisthenics, we got an alert to go to the field.
Colonel Phillips hadn't failed in even one respect! The helicopter
came into sight, hovered right over our army, then landed right
on the ball field! Out stepped the colonel with some recruiting
posters under his arm. He knew a golden opportunity when he
saw one, for we had a whole bunch of very available high school
seniors who were already in basic training!

With the staff in fatigues and walls decorated with recruiting posters of Uncle Sam pointing his finger at passersby, it was an unforgettable week. Each cabin company was charged with the responsibility—from the Word of God—to support their comrades in the battle. Their activities were creative as well as strenuous. How I wish you could have seen those kids riding on milk carton battleships in a water balloon sea battle, flying balsa wood aircraft on Air Force Day and singing, "I may never march in the infantry . . . !" Oh, how they sang!

In spite of the camp's huge success, I have discovered something that startles me back to reality: it takes more than a week of Bible camp to get spiritually prepared, equipped and disciplined to face the enemy. You must willingly reject worldliness and accept Jesus' call to be loyal, prepared and obedient. By doing so you will become a capable soldier who combats opponents with success because the Lord's army is *always* victorious!

A Soldier's Prayer

On December 8, 1984, a bittersweet anniversary was celebrated. It was on that date, 50 years earlier, that John and Betty Stam, a young missionary couple, gave their lives for the cause of Christ in China when they were beheaded.

When Betty Stam was just a young girl, and long before she began preparing to be a foreign missionary, she wrote a prayer that was found inscribed on the flyleaf of her Bible. Consider God's answer as you read it.

Lord,
I give up all my own plans and purposes,
All my own desires and hopes and accept Thy will for
    my life.
I give myself, my life, my all, utterly to Thee to be
    Thine forever.
Fill me and seal me with Thy Holy Spirit.
Use me as Thou wilt, Send me where Thou wilt,
Work out Thy whole will in my life at any cost, both now
    and forever. Amen.[6]

This is a soldier's prayer—to surrender to the will of the Commander. Can you pray that prayer and trust God for His answer in your life?

Give Us a Militant Spirit, Lord

Give us a militant spirit, Lord,
Come, set our spirits on fire.
Give us a passion to share Thy Word;
Give us consuming desire.

Give us a flaming and burning zeal
Moving us forward and on;
Help us the urgency, Lord, to feel
Till greater victory is won.

Help, dear Lord, all to volunteer
Time, talents, service and all.
Burn out indiff'rence, sloth and fear;
Challenge us with Thy call.

Baptize our souls with Thy holy love;
Yearn through us, love through our souls.
Center our vision on things above;
Banish all lesser earth-goals.

Give us a spirit of sacrifice
Help us to learn how to give;
Help us to love and forget the price,
Unselfishly help us live.

Teach us to value Thy Kingdom most
Putting our own int'rests last,
Send in a new way Thy Holy Ghost
Helping us often to fast.

Pray through us prayers that will shake the world,
Make us all warriors in prayer.
Keep us with banners of faith unfurled:
May we real prayer-battle share.

Help us a mighty offensive begin—
Forward for God on our knees!
Help us to conquer the hosts of sin
Praying for what Thou dost please.

Give us a militant spirit, Lord,
Banish indiff'rence and ease;
Help us advance and obey Thy Word,
NOW the offensive to seize.[7]

COMMISSIONS IN THE LORD'S ARMY

Who's in charge here?

Be here at the church by 5:00! Go to the committee meeting on Tuesday! Give! Pray! Sometimes even our Christian lives seem to be jammed with the stress caused by following someone else's orders! But when we get a proper perspective on our lives and service, we realize that we often need to have simple, direct commands to keep us alert. And God gives us all we need—with lots of room for personal adaptations within the framework of His instructions. He, who knows the beginning and end, has our best interests at heart and doesn't just throw us into the battle-field without a plan of attack developed around our particular equipment and capabilities.

Confront the Enemy

"This day I defy the ranks of Israel! Give me a man and let us fight each other" (1 Sam. 17:10, *NIV*). The Philistine's challenge rang out across the battleground in Judah. Goliath was at it again and the terrified brothers of David, a young shepherd boy, were among the quivering army of Israel. On that particular day David had just arrived to deliver a care package from home. He inquired as to what the commotion was all about and then rather naively asked the brave soldiers why someone hadn't taken Goliath at his challenge.

After learning of Goliath's grueling nature, David found his way to King Saul and volunteered to fight. Without wasting much time Saul responded to David by handing him his own armor. It was not exactly a one-size-fits-all outfit and little David rattled around in the king's personal defensive clothing!

Have you confronted any Goliaths lately?

How has God been preparing you for soldiering?

There are giant obstacles to service out there—like limited time for ministries you would love to be involved in, young children at home who need you so much, negative attitudes from other soldiers, or even a lack of proper equipment. How many other obstacles to service can you add to the list?

Perhaps you feel that all you bring to the battle is a loyalty to Christ and some experience in child rearing and Sunday School teaching, as well as membership in the women's organization and some skills retained from long-ago jobs. At first these weapons don't seem to fit as you confront the larger and more awesome challenge of doing battle against the sinful pressures on the family, the humanistic influences in education and the apathy that debilitates some churches. But like David, let's lay down the unfamiliar armor often given to us and dress ourselves in that which we are most accustomed—the armor of the godly woman which we have worn for years! May we stand with confidence in front of the enemy, using a battle cry that echoes David's famous words:

> "You come against me with sword and spear and javelin, but I come against you in the name of the Lord Almighty, the God of the armies of Israel, whom you have defied . . . . All those gathered here will know that it is not by sword or spear that the Lord saves; for the battle is the Lord's, and he will give all of you into our hands" (1 Sam. 17:45,47, *NIV*).

There is a certain amount of fear surrounding this command to confront, isn't there! After all, it is possibly a directive to risk personal comfort and face danger. But when faced with such an order, God gives us some unforgettable advice:

"Take [with me] your share of the hardships *and* suffering [which you are called to endure] as a good [first class] soldier of Christ Jesus. No soldier when in service gets entangled in the enterprises of [civilian] life; his aim is to satisfy *and* please the one who enlisted him" (2 Tim. 2:3-4, *AMP*).

Most of us know little about real suffering, for many of us serve in affluent churches. We don't pursue suffering or confrontation on any battlefront, and we desire the comfortable, convenient ministries! We struggle with our selfishness and words like obedience, loyalty and courage are hard ones to face. But take heart! The glorious truth of this message from the Word of God is that the One who enlisted you will provide you with all you need to please Him. He will give *courage* to *confront, power* to *pursue* the enemy, *equipment* for *effectiveness* and eventually the *victory*.

Recruit Others

Helping others to become involved and challenging women to service seems to be the most difficult part of leadership. Recruitment involves risk and your reputation is at stake. To enlist another is tantamount to endorsement of a project or ministry. The key is this: an effective recruiter is one who has already enlisted herself, wears the uniform of identification, has submitted to the disciplines of the project and is ready for anything.

The Bible is packed with battle accounts that give us some of God's principles for recruiting His armies. Let's look now at Judges 6 and 7 which records the Gideon story.

The angel of the Lord appeared to Gideon and announced to him that the Lord was with him and had a challenging new assignment meant only for him. After hedging—and going through some special object lessons for confirmation—Gideon was convinced he was still God's chosen leader! And what a battle lay ahead! The Midianites had literally reduced God's people to a frightened, destitute and bitter group of people. God had allowed them to be conquered because they had followed after other gods. But now, mercifully, the time had come for God to lead the Israelites into a much-needed victory. In the meantime the Midianites, who outnumbered the Israelites, were lolling about in leisure, confident that another victory was close at hand.

Gideon sent out a call for volunteers, as God has ordered, and 32,000 men responded!

"The army is too big!" responded the Lord.

"Too big? Lord, have you seen the Midianite army encamped down there? We need every warm body we can get!"

"Gideon, send home all those who are timid and frightened."

> Here is Principle One:
> *Invest your energies in the most effective place.*

Too much energy is spent trying to convince those who do not have a heart for the battle. Save your needed energy and spiritual strength for the battle itself.

It is hard to admit it, but had I heard Gideon's call, I would have probably left with that group of timid ones. We need to be sensitive to the fact that God's women have fears about the future, their capability to stand the test and the complications that invariably arise. For many *victory* isn't the issue—*survival* is. May the Lord make us into recruiters who are patient, courageous, kind, loving and sensitive to those who don't have the energy to fight the battle you are willing to engage in.

We must come to the point in our own ministry where we say, "God, help me to know the area in which you want me to fight." For example, you may feel that God is asking you to enlist the majority of God's women out there. Then, there's a battle and all kinds of excuses are offered:

"I have this situation at home."

"My priorities, you know."

"I'm too busy already."

You may be successful at calming the fears and hesitations of the many who *could* serve—but a battle always looms near. So, spend your energy equipping the smaller, already committed group for effective service, rather than cajoling the masses.

May I offer a practical illustration? Suppose you are the women's leader in your church. It is not too difficult to call a speaker of note, get a meeting on the church calendar and into the bulletin, arrange for some decorations and refreshments, have some fliers printed and recruit some music. It is not even difficult to enlist many to hear a speaker—particularly one with a dramatic "war story." But it *is* something else again, as many of you have already discovered, to ask a group of women to commit themselves to visiting a nursing home, to organize a youth retreat, or create a dynamite missions conference. For effectiveness in *all* areas of ministry, keep Principle One in mind. Be certain your energies are invested in the most effective place possible, even if it means that you have to gulp and send all the fainthearted home!

Now back to Gideon's story. We left off with God saying, "Now Gideon, send more of your volunteers home!"

"Lord!"

"Take them to the spring and observe the way they drink. One group will consist of men who cup the water in their hands to get it to their mouths. They will have their spears at their sides, poised and alert. The second group of men will lie down flat on their stomachs and lap the water from the streams like a dog." (See Judges 7:5.)

You know the result: only 300 of the men drank from their hands. All the others drank with their mouths in the stream.

This is Principle Two:
Release those who lie down and lap.

Let those go who are more concerned about their personal

needs and satisfaction than the defeat of the enemy just over the hill. Keep that small group—for Gideon just 300—who realize that they have needs but are willing to remain on the alert, with weapons poised. Work with that smaller group, that company of the committed.

"Lord, there are so many of them and so few of us!"

"Gideon, they have only weapons and battle strategy. I am going to give you the victory with a strategy that will confound them. You are going to fight this battle on my terms. You will fight with the strangest of all possible weapons—trumpets, torches and pitchers. In the middle of the night, with the army divided into three groups on the hills surrounding the enemy camp, you will shout and blow the trumpets. The pitchers will be smashed, the torches revealed and the night sky will be ablaze with fire."

"How will this give us the victory, Lord?"

"You won't even have to fight!"

The enemy was indeed confounded and reacted by killing each other.

There was no opportunity for Gideon to get any glory; the battle had been the Lord's from start to finish!

3

Principle Three:
*The closer you get to the battlefront,
the smaller the army should be.*

Let Principle Three become a confirmation that the Lord will fight for you rather than cause fear and trepidation. Work with that group, regardless of the number, and people who are qualified by reason of commitment and courage will enter the fray. Whether the projects involve scrubbing the church kitchen or helping rid the community of pornography, let the Lord fight for you!

Who will get the credit when a small group of you say, "Lord, we are ready to take the risk of serving you in leadership. It doesn't look like we are going to do very well, but—?" God will say, "Watch! I am setting you up so that you will realize it is 'not by might, nor by power, but by my Spirit' (Zech. 4:6, *NIV*) that you will get the victory. If you are willing to go in my power and give me all the glory, you will have a victory. And if you are careful to fight with the weapons of warfare that are not carnal, but mighty through me, you will win."

Take those women with questions in their minds and send them home for now. Take all those who are more concerned with their personal needs than the enemy who is close at hand and send *them* home for now. Another battle will be faced and perhaps then God will cause some to sense the urgency for training, and participation. For now, work with your select few and give God all the glory.

How to Inspire and Challenge Active Soldiering

1. Be sure the cause is worth fighting for and do not engage in busy work. Only invite others to a challenging, essential task.
2. Enlist yourself and let others sense your own commitment.
3. Realize there is a war. Communicate the urgency of the fight of faith.
4. Make a plan for basic training. Most women are unwilling to serve because they don't know how. A discipling ministry insures continuing leadership potential.
5. Plan ahead. Recruit for ministry far enough ahead of planned events so wise decisions can be made regarding involvement. Be sensitive about family concerns, holidays, etc.
6. Discharge the fainthearted. Allow those who haven't yet been spoken to by the Lord to wait for clearer direction. There is a tendency to spend energy, needed to carry out the Lord's commands, in convincing those fainthearted that there is a war!
7. Be specific when assigning job descriptions. When we are vague in our directions we frustrate our followers.
8. Evaluate strengths and weaknesses of the one you are

recruiting as well as the areas of need to be filled. Learn to observe attitudes and characteristics and recruit wisely so that each woman is convinced she is serving in her area of greatest effectiveness.

9. Challenge women to take risks and make some sacrifices. Help others to sense God's opportunity without playing God through manipulation.
10. Communicate enthusiasm and affirmation.
11. Never accept defeat. A negative, defeatist attitude is contagious. Do not communicate to others the reasons why some women are unable to serve. Be confidential and you will leave the door open to call when the time is better.

Create a poster or invitation to recruit help for an upcoming project or event. Ask yourself, what would get your attention?

✿ Rules for Recruiters

Attention! The battle is the Lord's and He will raise up an army of the concerned. Sometimes God uses just one and sometimes many. But no matter what the number, His Word offers principles to be followed when recruiting members for His army.

As you consider the following four battle situations from Scripture, can you identify some of the principles introduced earlier? Can you also spot some of God's commands?

1. *David and Goliath* (See 1 Samuel 17.)
   Principles:
   Commands:
2. *Gideon* (See Judges 7.)
   Principles:
   Commands:
3. *Esther* (See Esther 4-7.)
   Principles:
   Commands:
4. *Joshua* (See Joshua 1:8-9,16.)
   Principles:
   Commands:

STAND FIRM IN THIS EVIL DAY

"What can *one* person do?"

"Who would listen to me?"

"I don't have enough information to act intelligently."

"I don't think Christians should be involved in politics."

"We just turn off the television if something is on that we don't like."

Have you heard any or all of the above? Scripture records similar reasons—or excuses—for inactivity in the face of the enemy. If you have enlisted in the Army of the Lord, and

- dialogued with God as Moses did
- risked your royal position as Esther did
- dared to stake your life on God's promises as Daniel did or
- ventured forth with youth's enthusiasm as David did

then you know that God is willing to use our feeble selves on the daily front lines of our lives.

It was an ordinary spring day when I went to the local Safeway store to do some shopping. When I finally settled in at the end of the huge line to the checkout stand, my eyes began reading the headlines on the various magazines, almost subconsciously. Suddenly I saw *Playboy* in a new rack, situated at a height young and old could see, for sale directly to the right of the counter.

"When did *Playboy* get into Safeway?" I inquired when I finally reached the checker.

"Do you have a complaint to make? You will have to talk to the manager," the clerk declared.

"What seems to be the problem?" The manager seemed concerned about my query and suggested that I take a complaint card and send it to the "powers that be" for their consideration.

"May I have 50 of them?" I asked. "I am on my way to a women's Bible Study in this area and I think they will share my concern. You know, I am *certain* that you are not interested in having this magazine in your line and we do want to support you in this matter!" The gentleman gave me as many cards as he had. They were the same cards you fill out if your bacon is moldy or your eggs are rotten but I knew the Lord would use them in a great way.

A few weeks later, I received a letter from the supervisor of the Safeway Corporation. Expecting to find a form letter, I opened the envelope rather lackadaisically. But as I read I screamed with excitement!

"Thank you for expressing your concern. You will be glad to know that as a result of our consumer's reaction, the decision has been made against stocking *Playboy* and similar magazines in our California stores."

What a victory! Since we had first expressed our disapproval we had learned that the San Francisco Bay area was being used for a consumer's test to see if consumers would tolerate the presence of *Playboy* in the Safeway stores. How encouraging it was to discover that enough of us had registered our complaint to have convinced the management that we could not tolerate pornography being sold where we did our grocery shopping.

Women of God, where have we been? Some of us have spent years in holy huddles and behind the lines while the enemy of our homes has succeeded in infiltrating our neighborhoods with pornography, the television screen with a hedonistic value system and the schoolrooms with a humanistic curriculum. Child abuse, wife abuse and drug abuse are now among the major concerns of our society and we Christians must testify that we have the answer. The weapons needed to defeat the enemy have already been assigned to us!

Having gained such a significant victory over the fear in my own life when taking a stand, I went into the family drugstore located in the same shopping center and walked directly to the checkout stand. I was shocked to see not only *Playboy* and *Playgirl*, but *Penthouse, Oui,* and *Forum* magazines in a prominent place next to the counter. I went through the same process of talking to the manager and getting direction from him on how to register my complaint. Explaining again of my confidence that he was not interested in having the magazines in his store, I assured him that I would enlist the support of the women of our community to aid him in making his moral position clear to his superiors.

When I got back home I phoned the corporate headquarters and asked to speak to the president. I was finally connected to a vice-president and told him of my concerns.

"Well, Mrs. Hepburn, what would you like to see happen?"

"Mr. Gallo, I would like to see those responsible for the family retail corporations in our country take a stand that would indicate they are not willing to market materials that are below their personal moral standards. I would like to see moral courage exhibited by the leaders of your neighborhood chain of stores."

We talked for nearly 30 minutes. It was a long distance call and how grateful I was for his willingness to listen. I was disturbed, however, by some of his comments:

"We have millions of people in and out of our stores each week in Los Angeles County alone and we haven't received any complaints from them. And what would we tell people who come into our stores to purchase those magazines?"

"Sir, you can tell those customers the same thing you tell them when they come in looking for a fur coat or a dozen eggs: 'We don't carry them!'"

I inquired as to how many letters, phone calls or signatures it would take for the company to make a change in their policy regarding these questionable magazines. He assured me that everything would be all right—and I didn't need to "call out the troops" in this cause. "The troops" have kept up a correspondence, however, with some of us zeroing in on this one company with the hope that having a specific target, rather than sending just one or two complaints to each chain, would help. And it has to some extent. The magazines have been placed in opaque plastic bags and are supposedly only available to adults who ask for them. However, I am still convinced that if all the Christian soldiers in our one state alone, complained at the same time, in the same way, we would make a difference!

Can Just One Person Do Something?

After spending a day presenting a seminar to a group of women in a Northern California college town, I was exhausted and elated at the same time. The women had been *so* responsive as I challenged them to use 2 Timothy 2 as their basis for learning how to serve more effectively.

It was nearly a month later when I received a letter from one of the young married women who had attended that seminar.

And how my heart sang in praise to God! He had used one young woman's concern and sensitivity to make a difference in their community. Here's a copy of the letter Debbie received in response to her action:

Dear Mrs. Watkins:

I appreciate your taking the time to write and express your feelings about Shop 'N Save selling *Playboy* magazines. Mr. _____, the Manager of our _____ store, relayed your sentiments to me after his phone conversation with you and your follow-up letter reiterated the feelings you expressed to him.

I am pleased to tell you that as a direct result of your letter, we took immediate action on your complaint and pulled all *Playboy* and *Penthouse* magazines from our racks. This decision took place the same day your letter arrived in the office and our stores will no longer sell these two magazines.

I appreciate the positive comments you made about our store and its employees and I hope you will continue to be a Shop 'N Save customer. Thanks again, Mrs. Watkins, for taking the time to write and express your viewpoint on this matter. We really do respond to the wishes of our customers.

Sincerely yours,

(signed)

President

Isn't that encouraging? You see, there is something you can

do in the fight against pornography! May I suggest a few other guidelines to help in the battle.

1. Prayer is your most effective weapon.
2. Use courtesy and respect when speaking to store managers about questionable magazines.
3. Write to the headquarters of the stores when expressing your concern. Encourage others to do the same.
4. Use your buying power and stop shopping at these stores until they remove these magazines from their stores. This is my particular statement against pornography. As a matter of principle, I will not spend money in a store that cooperates with what is opposed to God's value system.
5. Cooperate with agencies that are collaborating to stamp out pornography. (See the resource list included at the end of this chapter.) For example, the National Federation of Decency set aside several days this last year to picket the stores in one chain, emphasizing the need to "clean up their act!" Join them!

A Minneapolis nurse and member of the Navigators decided that she had to do something with regard to the abortions that were being performed in the hospital where she worked. As a surgical nurse she often heard rumblings and complaints from others having to assist in the horror of abortions and she wanted to take positive action. She circulated a petition among the staff and presented the statement with accompanying names (nearly all who worked in the department) to the hospital administration. The result was a resounding victory for the pro-life cause! This is only one small hospital, in one city, located in our very big nation. But that particular hospital no longer does abortions and that is a victory for the Lord.

All over our land crisis pregnancy centers are being created as a scriptural alternative to abortion clinics. *You* can become a counselor and a volunteer in many areas. By doing this you'll become a soldier who is not only against something but is acting aggressively in favor of God's way.

Whether the issue is abortion or pornography, do you believe the Lord will lead you to take a stand in one or more specific areas if you ask Him by faith to use you?

How to Have a Moral Concerns Committee

1. *Find a few other people who are also concerned.*
   It is not necessary to have a large committee. Why not? Can you figure it out? The larger the committee, the more difficult it is to convene. Remember the Gideon principles!

2. *Convene a meeting and choose a chairman.*
   You will soon find that having a designated leader is the only way your committee can function effectively. Getting together for sharing sessions soon loses appeal. There needs to be an accountability to each other and to the leader that gives form and shape to your committee. The Chairman should:
   a. Convene all meetings
   b. Keep a calendar and coordinate it
   c. Perhaps sit on the board of your women's ministry or parent organization.

3. *Select four specific areas of concern.*
   First make a list of all the concerns that seem to need urgent attention or action. Please note that there will be many and the list will increase as the committee is exposed to the legislative trends, the news media and current events pieces available. Choose four or five of the issues which the group considers to be priority for the next 12 months.

4. *Each committee member assumes responsibility for one area to research.*
   When the committee gets together the leader will guide the group through the research and encourage a position description to be written on each concern. It is then important to develop a specific plan for action that may include a letter-writing campaign, a telephone alert, insert for the church bulletin, a picketing party, etc. It is not necessary to discuss the evils of pornography each time the group meets for there to be enough motivation and preparation to correct the problem!

5. *Create a calendar of action.*
   Such calendars will no doubt include mini conferences, prayer breakfasts, mailings and petitions.

6. *Remember Nehemiah!*
   God's people were hard at work because the walls were broken down and the gates around Jerusalem were burned. The enemy was attacking because something was being accomplished in the name of the Lord! The people were afraid and Nehemiah got them organized. Then, after he had given each person a place to work and defend themselves, he encouraged them:

> Don't be afraid of them. Remember the Lord, who is great and awesome, and fight for your brothers, your sons and your daughters, your wives and your homes (Neh. 4:14, *NIV*).

Resource List

1. Television and pornography

   National Federation of Decency
   P.O. Box 1398
   Tupelo, MS 38802

2. A general concerns newsletter

   Intercessors for America
   P.O. Box D
   Elyria, OH 44036

3. Textbooks

   Educational Research Analysis
   Attn: Mel and Norma Gabler
   P.O. Box 7518
   Longview, TX 75602

4. Family concerns

   Concerned Women for America
   Attn: Beverly LaHaye
   122 C St. NW
   Suite 800
   Washington, D.C. 20001

   Focus on the Family
   Attn: James Dobson
   P.O. Box 500
   Arcadia, CA 91006

5. National concerns	Washington Insight National Association of Evangelicals P.O. Box 28 Wheaton, IL 60187
6. Pornography	Morality in Media 475 Riverside Drive New York, New York 10027
	Christian Action Council 422 C St. NE Washington, D.C. 20002

You will also find that there is an encouraging trend in several Christian magazines to treat moral issues and their impact on Christians. Much help is offered for victims, as well as resources made available for those in ministry who want to help others.

Recommended reading: *The High Cost of*
Indifference
Edited by Richard Cizik
Published by Regal Books

While women weep, as they do now,
I'LL FIGHT;
while little children go hungry, as they do now,
I'LL FIGHT;
while men go to prison, in and out,
in and out, as they do now,
I'LL FIGHT;
while there is a poor lost girl
upon the streets,
while there remains one dark soul
without the light of God,
I'LL FIGHT;
I'll fight to the very end![8]

PORTRAIT OF A SOLDIER

I have a heritage of soldiering. Both my parents and my in-laws—as well as my husband David and I for a time—were officers of The Salvation Army. The Army has been a part of my life, for all of my life, and those *S's* worn on the Salvationist's lapels are significant. Not only do they identify the organization but symbolize the "Saved to Serve" slogan of the Army's ministry. One Salvationist who wore the *S* in a particularly noble way was the founder's wife, Catherine Booth. I have read and reread her biography, and she was a fine soldier of Jesus Christ. I'd like to share with you these words from her story:

> Let us stand together by her open grave in the autumn twilight. Her twenty-six years of fight and toil in The Salvation Army are over now, her spirit has been summoned Home. Listen. The Army Founder himself is the speaker. He is recalling the forty years which he and our dear Army Mother had trod together, and his words sum up better than any other words could do what she was to our Leader:
>
> "If you had had a tree" he said, speaking to the vast crowd that stood round the grave, "that had grown up in your garden, under your window, which for forty years had been your shadow from the burning sun, whose flowers had been the adornment and beauty of your life, whose fruit had been almost the stay of your existence, and the gardener had come along and swung his glittering axe and cut it down before your eyes, I think you would feel as though you had a blank—it might not be a big one—but a little blank in your life.
>
> "If you had had a servant who for all this long time had served you without fee or reward, who had administered for very love, to your health and comfort, and who suddenly passed away, you would miss that servant.
>
> "If you had had a counsellor who, in hours—continually occurring—of perplexity and amazement, had ever advised you, and seldom advised wrong; whose

advice you had followed, and seldom had reason to regret it; and the counsellor, while you were in the same intricate mazes of your existence, had passed away, you would miss that counsellor.

"If you had had a friend who had understood your very nature, the rise and fall of your feelings, the bent of your thoughts, and the purpose of your existence; a friend whose communion had ever been pleasant—the most pleasant of all other friends—to whom you had ever turned with satisfaction, and your friend had been taken away, you would feel some sorrow at the loss.

"If you had had a wife, a sweet love of a wife, who for forty years had never given you real cause for grief; a wife who had stood with you, side by side, in the battle's front, who had been a comrade to you, ever willing to interpose herself between you and the enemy, and ever the strongest when the battle was fiercest, and your beloved one had fallen before your eyes, I am sure there would be some excuse for your sorrow.

"Well, my comrades, you can roll all these qualities into one personality, and what would be lost in all I have lost in one. There has been taken away from me the light of my eyes, the inspiration of my soul, and we are about to lay all that remains of her in the grave. I have been looking right at the bottom of it here, calculating how soon they may bring and lay me alongside of her, and my cry to God has been that every remaining hour of my life may make me readier to come and join her in death, to go and embrace her in life in the Eternal City."

May we be given such a eulogy when we have finished our soldiering. And may we be the kind of comrade and warrior the Lord calls us to be. It's a noble cause and one that will produce glorious victories for our One True Commander.

 Sword Drill

Are you old enough to remember when the Sunday School superintendent counted the Bibles brought? After the count we would then have a Sword Drill. I seem to remember the instructions going something like this: "Attention!" We would all sit on the edges of our chairs, backs ramrod straight. We each raised our tightly closed Bibles into the air. "John 3:17—strike" (any verse was OK)! The first one of us on our feet, ready to read the verse, received an insignia on the target placed up front. Perhaps this game sounds outdated and old-fashioned, but I dare say that many of us wouldn't do all that well in a verse search contest, even with our technological approaches to information.

I challenge you to try it for yourself. Look up these references in the Bible and see how many you know by heart but couldn't find unless given some direction. Make a note of them for future Sword Drills.

Reference	Command
Joshua 1:9	
Deuteronomy 6:5	
Exodus 20:12	
Matthew 7:12	
John 13:34	
Galatians 5:1	
Ephesians 6:10	

❀ The Believer's Armor

This spiritual clothing, to be put on each morning, is guaranteed to resist stains, shrinkage and even tears imposed by the evil one!

1. The belt of truth (see Eph. 6:14) deals with our problem of confusion.
   The Word of God in the mind (see 2 Tim. 2:15), in the heart (see Josh. 1:8) and in the way (Ps. 119:9).
2. The breastplate of righteousness (see Eph. 6:14) deals with our problem of guilt.
   A life-style patterned after Christ's (see Eph. 4:22-32).
3. The shoes of peace and witness (see Eph. 6:15) deals with our problem of purposelessness.
   Daily preparation to share Jesus Christ (see 1 Pet. 3:15).

4. The shield of faith (see Eph. 6:16) deals with the problem of temptation.
   Undisturbed confidence in the promise of God (see 1 Cor. 10:13).
5. The helmet of salvation (see Eph. 6:17) deals with our problem of doubt.
   An understanding of God's simple plan of salvation (see 1 John 5:10,15).
6. The sword of the Spirit (see Eph. 6:17) deals with our problem of attitude.
   Application of the Word of God to conscience (see Heb. 4:12).
7. Prayer (see Eph. 6:18) deals with our problem of powerlessness.
   Careless prayer can lose a battle.

C-Rations or Enough Pizza Burgers
to Feed an Army of 50

    3 lbs. hamburger, browned
    1 can Spam, grated
    2 lbs. grated cheddar cheese
    1 can of spaghetti sauce mix
 ½ cup grated onion
 ¼ tsp. sage
    1 tsp. oregano
    1 tsp. basil

Pizza Toppings:
olives
pepperoni
mozzarella etc.
2½ doz. hamburger buns

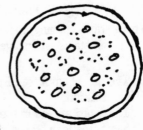

Mix together and spread on half of the buns. Bake 12 minutes at 425 degrees. Top with your choice of pizza toppings during the last five minutes.

Everyday Armor

Look on your Believer's Armor Worksheet and list the pieces of armor used by the Christian soldier. Now, look around your own home. Can you find some everyday, practical coordinates?

Armor	*Household Item*
1. Belt of Truth	1. A belt for your new dress that gives support as well as color and accent.
2.	
3.	
4.	
5.	
6.	
7.	

Moses led the children of Israel into victory after the attack by the Amalekites. It was certainly a cooperative victory, for Moses stayed up on the hill with his rod raised. As long as the rod was held high, the Israelites were winning. But when the rod slipped down because of fatigue, God's army began to be overtaken.

Joshua was the swordbearer, but his winning depended on Moses' support. That's the way it is with most of us—we *really* do need each other. Some of us will fight as intercessors, with our hands raised in prayer, while others of us will be on the battlefield involved in hand-to-hand combat.

Let's be careful to do what Moses and Joshua did—and that is to cooperate instead of compete with one another.

Do you remember what Moses did next? He built an altar and named it "God Is My Flag" or "The Lord Is My Banner."

When my parents retired to a little home in the lovely hills of Pennsylvania, Dad already had a flagpole set in cement on their front lawn. Our family presented them with a family flag, designed just for them and to fly beneath the stars and stripes daily. Mother has gone to heaven and Dad is in a retirement home, so I have the flag here for a while. It was made of Salvation Army colors—yellow, red and blue—and has a family insignia in the center. God is our banner, too.

Joshua called out to the people before He went to heaven and challenged them to choose. Why not make a family flag for your home and use that memorable verse:

"As for me and my household, we will serve the Lord" (Josh. 24:15, *NIV*).

Look, You're an Athlete!

KNOWING THE RULES

"Follow the Lord's rules for doing his work, just as an athlete either follows the rules or is disqualified and wins no prize" (2 Tim. 2:5, *TLB*).

One year my husband and I invested in a membership at a local health club—but soon realized it was too crowded for our enjoyment. Last year we bought a home-sized "bouncer" which the makers claimed was all we needed in athletic equipment to get into shape. (Now if I can only remember what shape we're trying to get back into!) This year we purchased a rowing machine which took up residence in the living room. In spite of our good intentions it has become more of a conversation piece than a daily part of our lives. It has also become a nagging symbol of our lack of motivation.

Recall the 1984 Olympic Games! How we marveled at the discipline, commitment, beauty and thrill of our athletes in competition. At such occasions we are forced to admit that we are "over the hill" and will never be awarded a gold medal, hear the national anthem played in our honor or receive flower bouquets because of our athletic achievements! And perhaps it is with a sigh of relief that we read in the Word of God that spiritual fitness rather than physical fitness is the most important goal for our lives.

Since we, as women of God, are called to participate in spiritual workouts, we had better take this call seriously as well as know the rules. Let me share a story that will show you the penalty for playing in ignorance.

The Victor's Crown

"It's time to sign up for this afternoon's tennis round-robin," the voice of the program director boomed across the dining room. My husband and I were attending a summer conference and were eager to cooperate with the proposed schedule. David and I really don't have tennis built into our lives, but we signed up anyway! Whatever made me do it I will never know.

After I put on my J.C. Penney culottes and navy blue sneakers, and David donned his Montgomery Ward work pants, we proceeded up the hill. I clutched my racquet tightly because the tape was unraveling from the handle. (Can you expect authentic catgut and suede tape from a discount house?)

Our names were called and we gallantly skipped onto our assigned court. For the first time I could really see the other participants and I felt psychologically defeated! The women wore tiny, white pleated skirts and had pompoms on their pure white tennis shoes (theirs were definitely *not* sneakers). Their hair was coiffed beneath cute white visors that matched those worn by their husbands. I was just trying to be a good sport and could not have been more relieved when the chief robin (is that what they call the scorekeeper?) indicated that we had lost!

When the bulk of the crowd wound their way back down the hill David and I met at the net. "How about if you and I just play around and try to hit the ball *to* each other. Let's see how many times we can get it over the net without stopping!"

We worked up to nine consecutive hits and were hot but elated at the progress. There was one big drawback, however. Can you figure out what it was? The game soon lost its fascination because neither of us knew if the other had won or lost—we *didn't know the rules!*

I can get out onto the court, bat the ball back and forth, and look like I am playing the game. There might, in fact, even be a few novice onlookers who could be convinced that I was winning. But unless I apply myself to learning and obeying the rules, I will never win and never receive the victor's crown.

The Scripture teaches us that there are rules for God's athlete, and if we are to be qualified for the prize we must subject ourselves to the training and day-to-day discipline necessary for the game.

Do you know what my husband gave me for Christmas? A tennis dress! It was the most ridiculous looking thing and was one size too small, but how I loved him for dreaming big dreams and setting high goals! I had to return it, along with the matching panties, to the exclusive little tennis shop in which he had bought it. Now, could I wear lace-trimmed briefs that had *Tennis Mom?* embroidered across them? The salespeople were not interested in my story, why the dress didn't fit or much else to do with me. But when the young clerk suggested that I exchange the panties for another pair in my size with the words, *Wanna Cheat?* written across them, it was the last straw!

Now I have a nice, conservative, navy cotton-blend tennis dress. Should I ever have the courage to appear on a tennis court again, I'll have something to wear. I'll also pay closer attention to the rules so I can be a legitimate player—and hopefully, a winner.

It is good exercise to list some of the rules given to us in the Word. Take Ephesians 4 and 5, for example. Can you find the rules that are there in the suggested verses? Think about how they might have a part in your spiritual fitness regimen.

Ephesians 4:22 _____

4:23 _____

4:26 _____

4:28 _____

4:29 _____

4:30 _____

4:31 _____

4:32 _____

5:1 _____

5:3 _____

Let us be athletes who strive for masteries over ourselves, according to the rules.

A Will to Win

Shortly after my summer conference tennis experience a size-five friend offered to include me in a group tennis lesson she was coaching. It was there I learned that some tennis balls are alive and some are dead. Likewise, the servant-athlete is characterized by a will to win. But there is a philosophy in our society that competition is a no-no, for if there is a winner then there will be a loser. And nobody likes to be a loser or to be labeled a loser. However, who does the Scripture tell us is to be our opponent? Against whom are we to compete? Over what are we to gain mastery?

The answer may surprise you because it is ourselves! We are not to compete against other Christians for power or prizes; we are to measure our progress against ourselves. The Lord also teaches us that personal satisfaction with "how far we have come" or "how well we are doing" is *never* satisfactory—we are to continually press on, looking forward, being transformed:

> Now every athlete who goes into training conducts himself temperately *and* restricts himself in all things . . . . But [like a boxer] I buffet my body—handle it roughly, discipline it by hardships—and subdue it, for fear that after proclaiming to others the Gospel *and* things pertaining to it, I myself should become unfit—not stand the test and be unapproved" (1 Cor. 9:25,27, *AMP*).

That desire to win must also be willing to compete against the forces of evil! We must be in condition to struggle and compete not against other people, "For our struggle is not against flesh and blood, but against the rulers, against the powers, against the world forces of this darkness, against the spiritual *forces* of wickedness in the heavenly *places*" (Eph. 6:12, *NASB*).

Competition is scriptural—but let us be careful and know what the Word says about the rules to be followed when competing against our opponents.

Athletes in Action

In 2 Timothy 2:5, Paul concentrates on the preparation and qualification of the individual for competition. He speaks of the discipline necessary to achieve the goal and the necessity of playing according to the rules if the prize is to be won. So must we be like the Greek athlete who was required to subject himself to 10 months of rigorous training before he was qualified to enter the race or competition. The competitor who was not willing to get the proper exercise, rest or diet not only did not get the crown but lowered the standard of the whole game.

> Therefore, since we have so great a cloud of witnesses surrounding us, let us also lay aside every encumbrance, and the sin which so easily entangles us, and let us run with endurance the race that is set before us, fixing our eyes on Jesus, the author and perfecter of faith (Heb. 12:1-2, *NASB*).

 Are You Following the Rules?

1. Meditate on 1 Corinthians 9:24-27 and Philippians 3:1-16 concerning the attitude of Paul's heart and his priorities. List the things Paul laid aside in order to run his "race."

2. Prayerfully consider any area of your life that is hindering your effectiveness as a child of God. Count it as sin and ask God to give you victory over it, even if the process is difficult or uncomfortable.*

GO BEYOND YOURSELF

Bev is a young mom in excellent physical condition who probably wears a size five (which I personally think should be against the law!). A few years ago she decided she needed some exercise and she bounded out of her South Minneapolis front door just as her husband was coming in for supper. Exhilarated with positive action from her afternoon decision, Bev waved and was off. She ran two blocks and collapsed on the sidewalk.

Stay with it! said a strange voice from inside. And she did—working up to a few blocks and even a mile as the days went by.

Now—around a lake. See all the neighbors looking at the funny lady running while her kids cheer her on . . . see Bev run! The snow falls, and Bev keeps running; springtime arrives, and Bev runs on.

Eventually Boston Marathon became a tantalizing goal—but could she make it? There were qualifications to meet and grueling longer distances to be gained daily.

Finally April arrived and Bev went to Boston. With gleeful determination she looked forward to achieving her goal. What had been a long-term goal now appeared on her near horizon. She had followed the rules and now came the test. She proudly bore a Minnesota banner across her chest and a number on her back for identification. Her husband and children cooled the Gatorade.

Excitement mounted and then peaked as the starting gun was fired. Thousands of participants ran the people-lined streets. Bev waved and smiled at the encouragers—at least for the first several miles. It is said by many that the 26 miles of the marathon run is beyond the limit of human endurance, but Bev

*
(Adapted with permission from WORLDWIDE CHALLENGE—Campus Crusade for Christ, Inc., (1978). All rights reserved.

finished—perhaps after twilight, I don't know—but she ran the race and achieved her goal!

Did she win? That's a matter of viewpoint, don't you think? If you ask, "Did she come in first?" Then, of course, the answer is no. But if you mean, "Did she finish the course?" the answer is a resounding YES!

Later on Bev shared that there were times during those last miles when the thought crept in, *Why am I doing this? Nobody said I had to go through this! I just want to die!* But she won the prize of knowing that she had reached far down inside and had grasped onto the understanding of what it is like to live beyond one's own capacity.

She ran the race again the next year—and the next. And running daily has become part of her own discipline and regimen. For each marathon she runs she has the goal of bettering her previous time. She wants to do better, run harder and compete against herself!

> I am still not all I should be but I am bringing all my energies to bear on this one thing: Forgetting the past and looking forward to what lies ahead, I strain to reach the end of the race and receive the prize for which God is calling us up to heaven because of what Christ Jesus did for us (Phil. 3:13-14, *TLB*).

Now that's a prize—the real goal to be won! "Yes, everything else is worthless when compared with the priceless gain of knowing Christ Jesus my Lord" (Phil. 3:8, *TLB*).

Go for the Gold

To be God's servant-athlete we must have a clear goal in mind. Let's think back on Bev. Why did she keep on running? No one was whipping her. And was the world any different because one young mother was "pressing toward a mark?" Why did she not just give up? Actually, she hadn't a breath of a chance of winning the race.

At the nineteenth mile Bev often tells that she came to the end of herself. Is that part of the achievement of aiming for

God's highest goals in our lives? Are we to come to the end of ourselves? Are we to acknowledge that we will not be able to finish using our own strength? I believe that it is at those moments that God is able to release His power to do for us what we cannot do for ourselves.

More often than not we Christian women drop out because of our feelings of inadequacy in personal relationships, in personal discipline or in our leadership roles. We say over and over again, "We are not able." God says, "I knew it all along. Begin to appropriate my supernatural power and trust me when I say you 'shall walk and not faint'" (see Isa. 40:31).

My prayer is that the Lord will give me a touch of that supernatural power in my life. I am sick of the insipid existence that involves only what I know I can do. I want to reach out, set higher goals and experience what it means to depend on the resources of my God. I want these things for you, too, so let's ask the Lord to help us establish priorities, which, when consistently followed, will enable us to reach worthier goals.

> In a race, everyone runs but only one person gets first prize. So run your race to win. To win the contest you must deny yourselves many things that would keep you from doing your best. An athlete goes to all this trouble just to win a blue ribbon or a silver cup, but we do it for a heavenly reward that never disappears. So I run straight to the goal with purpose in every step (1 Cor. 9:24-26, *TLB*).

More Than Semantics

Bev had a goal.

The disciple Paul also had a goal, a mark, a prize for which he was willing to expend all his energies: the priceless gain of knowing Christ.

Perhaps we are just playing a game of semantics, but then again, as we consider some well-used words, I'm confident you will gain a small prize in the form of a new insight into worthy targets and goals for your own life.

Take the word PURPOSE, for example. What is the purpose

of your life? Right! To glorify God and enjoy Him forever. How do you fulfill that purpose? The Scripture teaches that there are many ways to glorify God: with our praise (see Ps. 50:23); with our witness (see Matt. 5:16); in our suffering (see Rom. 8:17).

Next, think about COMMITMENT. If you have accepted God's highest and holiest purpose for your life—that of bringing glory to God, you have committed yourself first to Him, and second to what the Lord Jesus expects of you. How thankful you can be that your commitment to the Lord does not conflict with your commitment to your family—whatever form that family takes in your life. Are you a wife, a widow? Do you have children of your own? Or are your children those that you teach day-to-day in a school classroom? Those who make up your family are a God-given gift to help you to live out your commitment to the Lord in daily ways.

You have additional commitments to the family of God (in your church and peripheral ministries) and then to the work of God. That work—your work—is also God's work, regardless of whether it is done behind your front door, in your church, in the city mission, in the office or behind the counter. Your commitment to Jesus Christ encompasses all other commitments of your life.

Now consider GOALS. Can you think of the differences between a goal and a purpose or commitment? Ed Dayton and Ted Engstrom, in their book *Strategy for Living,* helped me by providing some helpful definitions: "A purpose is an aim or direction, something which we want to achieve, but something which is not necessarily measurable. A goal, on the other hand, is a future event which we believe is both accomplishable and measurable."[1] You know when your goal has been reached.

Let's investigate a fourth word—PRIORITIES. Priorities are what you do to realize your goals, because of your commitment to fulfill your purpose. Let me illustrate. My purpose is to glorify God. One of the ways I do this is to keep my body under subjection and in good condition. Would you believe that a year or so ago I was 20 pounds overweight? I have been playing lost and found with that same 20 pounds for 20 years! Well, I set a goal to lose those 20 pounds. And after calling a local weight loss support group, I enrolled (kicking and screaming inside). I set a goal date for the weight loss and set out to achieve the goal by making attendance at that class a priority. I had to be consistent as well as allow for a measurable amount of time to lapse.

Tell me that you have experienced the thrill of reaching a goal weight! I will not inquire as to how long you stayed there, but life is full of small victories and this was one of mine!

Being a "Both-And" Woman

It is not possible to measure the personal fulfillment gained when we meet a deadline on our calendar or see a reduction on our scales, but I certainly know when I have reached a goal. And it is when our priorities are not in line with the fulfillment of our definite goals that we become frustrated.

One of the reasons for frustration in my own very busy life is trying to pigeon-hole the activities of my day. There is too much compartmentalizing. Sometimes when I am shopping for groceries my mind is flooded with all the other aspects of my day: preparing for a meeting, typing for my husband or dealing with the frustration of spending such a brief time with the Lord. At these moments the Lord brings calm to me by whispering simply, "Daisy, I will help you to be a 'both-and' and not an 'either-or.'" Because of my life's purpose and my basic commitments, I must wear several hats. Many times the Lord shows me how those priorities can be flexible and balanced simultaneously with my commitments.

One of my goals is to see my children grow into maturity in Jesus and to be occupied in His service, whatever their occupation. This is not the purpose for which I live, but it is a goal because of my commitment.

Given this goal, my next step is to order the activity of my life, to prioritize, so my goal will be achieved. One of my priorities must be prayer! Another for me might be to bring some extra income into our home to help support our daughter who attends a Christian college. Perhaps you work for a Christian organization serving the community. Can you see how working out our commitments to God, to our families, to His family, and to His work can occur all at the same time?

Instead of visualizing these words in a list, how about using this design for clarification:

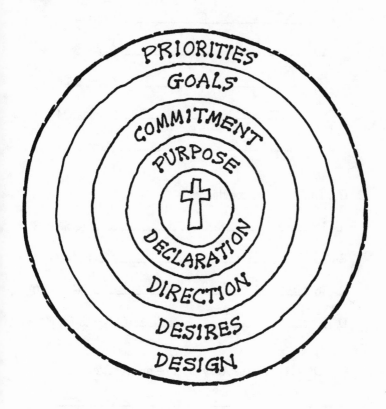

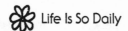 Life Is So Daily

"So teach *us* to number our days, that we may apply *our* hearts unto wisdom" (Ps. 90:12, *KJV*, italics added).

1. Our DECLARATION or purpose:

   _____ (Isa. 43:7)

   How? _____ (Matt. 5:16)

   _____ (Rom. 15:6)

   _____ (John 11:4)

   _____ (Rom. 8:17)

2. Our DIRECTION or commitment:

   A. To _____ (Col. 1:18)

   B. To _____ (Eph. 5:21-6:4)

   C. To _____ (Gal. 6:10)

   D. To _____ (Col. 3:23-24, *KJV*)

3. Our DESIRES or goals: they must be measurable.

   _____

   _____ (Ps. 37:4)

   Is there a difference between dreams and desires?

   How must my desires (goals) fulfill my commitments?

4. Our DESIGN or priorities: they must be flexible to fulfill measurable goals. Simply stated, our first priority is to do first what only we can do. Here are some good examples:

- Only *you* can be a wife to your husband
- Only *you* can spend time with the Lord
- Only *you* can be mother to your children.

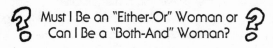

Must I Be an "Either-Or" Woman or Can I Be a "Both-And" Woman?

You can answer the question above by taking a few minutes to confirm your commitments. Begin by listing just one. (Should you want to list others, repeat the exercise.)

My commitment: _____

Now set your goals. You may want to look back on the material to insure that you're setting goals and not listing purposes.

One long-term goal: _____

One short-term goal: _____

Note some priorities (what you do) that will enable you to meet your long-term and short-term goals:

_____

_____

_____

As you make this ordering of your life second nature, as you bring your life under simplest direction and as you get into shape you will experience the joy and exhilaration of accomplishment—something like running a marathon!

"As thy days, *so shall* thy strength *be*" (Deut. 33:25, *KJV*, italics added).

Choosing the High Hill

One of the dangers we must face as an athlete-leader is setting our goals too low. Have you had a tendency to get discouraged because of mediocrity? Busy work? Your goals are too low. Let the goals for your ministry and service be lofty and excellent ones to fulfill the purposes of God. Go for gold.

"This year we are going to have five combined meetings," announced a woman in one of my seminars. Why? The answer was slow in coming because the goals for their meetings were indefinite. Just *meeting* is not an adequate goal. What do you want to see happen? What will you ask God to do for you and all who attend?

Programming without goals does not constitute a ministry. And an activity or filling up the calendar is not synonymous with success. We tend to fulfill our goals when some tension is applied. Even a rubber band is good for nothing unless stretched.

You have the highest possible purpose—to give God glory. Set high goals and bring your priorities in line to achieve those goals. It is then that God will get glory from your plans, your preparation, your product.

In my book, *Why Doesn't Somebody Do Something?* I quote my husband. It's worth including here as well. When I am tempted to expend energies in trivia and run around in circles with things or situations that just don't matter and are not contributing to the goal, David says, "Daisy, that is just not a high enough hill to die on." May this come to mind as we choose activities that are aimed at giving God the glory.

❀ Prioritizing for Servant-Leadership

The Scriptures are full of guidelines for establishing priorities. Following is a list of references dealing with our time, our money and our abilities. Do a little mental gymnastics and decide which category each might relate to:

Time	Money	Abilities

Proverbs 11:24-25

Proverbs 15:6,16-17,19

Proverbs 16:8-9

Proverbs 17:1

Proverbs 19:15,17,21

Proverbs 20:4,7

Malachi 3:6-10

Matthew 6:19-34

Luke 15:3-16:31

Romans 12:9-13

1 Corinthians 16:2

2 Corinthians 9:6-15

Ephesians 5:15-16

Philippians 2:4-11

Hebrews 13:1-6

Exercising Priorities

1. In Hebrews 13:1-6 note the verbs (those actions words!) and the areas of our lives to which they refer. Is this list a priority list or do you think it needs to be reordered?

2. The virtuous woman of Proverbs 31 has a variety of priorities. Can you list those in order (at least six) and see how the list compares to one of your own? See Proverbs 31:10-31.

   Now look *back* 10 years and compare how your list might have looked for your life in that season.

   As you look *ahead* 10 years or even 20 years, how might your priority list have to be adapted and kept flexible?

3. Psalm 37 instructs us in day-by-day training with the promise of God's strength. List at least eight rules from this chapter and try to locate a corresponding promise from the same Psalm.

Rule	Verse
1.	
2.	
3.	
4.	
5.	
6.	
7.	
8.	

CONSIDER COACHING YOUR TEAM

Some of the most agonizing moments of the Olympic Games involved watching the emotions bursting out in grins and grimaces on the faces of the coaches for the athletes performing. And how often the camera shows the reactions of the coach—restricted to the sidelines—as in a football game. Regardless of his proximity, the coach is a great part of the game and his advice and training often accounts for the success—or failure—of the team.

Although I don't mind dispensing advice—often without even an invitation to do so and sometimes without knowing much about the situation—there hasn't been much call for my service in the field of professional athletics. But athletes need coaches and Scripture calls some women to fill this role. It appears that in the Body of Christ there is a deep need for women who are willing to help other women.

The Lord has granted me a precious privilege. Each year I meet and visit with many, many women at retreats and conferences. So much of what we talk about, the problems and challenges now faced, even in Christian homes, could be measurably eased and even solved if there were women willing to listen and coach using scriptural principles.

Most of us will never become full-time counselors, but any of you who are willing to go a bit beyond can become a people-helper or coach.

Let's look and see what are the eight *C*'s to being an effective coach:

Confidential

A coach must be able to keep a confidence. (See Prov. 6:16-19.)

You have heard that there are three means of communication: telephone, telegraph and tell-a-woman! We women as a whole have not had a good image because many of us have been unable to keep a secret or a confidence. The old gossip has been just that—a game—all too often.

Bursting to tell a juicy morsel? Why, we've even been known

to use a prayer meeting as a spiritual cloak for this weakness in our character:

> Tonight I would appreciate prayer for Barbara. It is not necessary for me to share all the details. Just remember to pray for her family and that the Lord will intervene before they need to go for professional help. Pray that circumstances will be reversed so love and communication can begin in their home.

What goes on in your mind? Any additions to that "prayer request" are up to the hearer's imagination—and most of us are good at that. May the Lord forgive us for making our prayers news bulletins.

Be wary, too, of "sharing sessions" that give out too much information to be carefully handled. We are awfully human, after all! You will find women are less and less willing to share their lives if that is what is required and expected at your Bible study groups. Vulnerability is important, but time is required to establish that rapport in a group setting.

Compassionate

A coach is compassionate. (See 1 John 3:17.)

Except I am moved with compassion
How dwellest Thy Spirit in me?
In word and in deed
Burning love is my need
I know I can find this in Thee.[2]

The dictionary says that compassion is sympathy and tenderheartedness. Therefore a compassionate coach must develop an ear that listens to understand and not to criticize. What is the need? Whether it be permanent help or temporary relief, may your motive always be to listen with a tender heart.

Little Janie came into the house and told her mother that her friend Susie had dropped her doll and it had broken.

"Did you help her fix it?" Janie's mother asked.

"No, we couldn't fix it," replied Janie, "but I helped her cry!"

Most of us will probably never hang out a counselor's shingle but let's at least help one another cry!

Conscientious

A coach will be conscientious to stand on principle regardless of preference or pressure. (See Ps. 119:4; Josh. 1:7-8).

In an article in *Moody Monthly* entitled "Let's Let Women Counsel Women," Naomi Taylor Wright shares some truths from the Lord that should be in your coaching rule book:

1. Pastors should create the opportunity for godly older women in their congregations to teach and counsel younger women.

2. Such a woman must really know God's Word, not be judgmental and be able to speak the truth in love. She may be an older woman whose family is grown and gone or she may be a younger woman who is spiritually mature—"older" in Christ.

3. She must be one who loves her husband and home, is compassionate toward others and is accustomed to bearing spiritual fruit. She must be teachable herself.

4. She must know how to introduce people to Christ and how to use God's Word in counseling. She must believe in the permanency of marriage. She must believe that scriptural principles work and that God is the "God of hope."[3]

Principles are fundamental laws of eternal and changeless truths that can serve as a guide for conduct or procedure. You will be on very dangerous ground if you allow your personal preferences to enter the helping situation. It is coaching through principles—the principles of the Word—that stands the test of time. Rev. James Braga says that principles have several features:

1. Each is a positive, not a negative statement.
2. Each is a clear or incisive declaration.
3. Each is a truth that is always valid.
4. Each is an established law, basic for life and conduct.[4]

If this is all true, could it be that there are conflicting principles in the Word? No. A basic knowledge of the Word is helpful—but so is skill in searching the Word when the principle doesn't trip off your tongue. Do not be intimidated into inactivity because you feel inadequate in this area. I believe it was Mrs. Billy Graham that I heard say one day when I was privileged to hear her speak, "Have a message and God will give you ministry." Ask the Lord for a deeper desire to really *know* His Word and He will give you opportunity to use it.

Back to the question of conflict. There are those who play games with the Word, even when helping others, by citing a verse or a passage, out of context, so it will appear as a principle. Second Timothy 2:15 states that we are to be studied workmen in order to show ourselves approved unto God. Likewise we are never to be ashamed that we are correctly handling the Word of Truth. Manipulating the Scripture so it will say something that was not intended is wrongly handling the Word.

For instance, Jesus is speaking to a crowd in Matthew 5:38, *TLB*:

> The law of Moses says, "If a man gouges out another's eye, he must pay with his own eye. If a tooth gets knocked out, knock out the tooth of the one who did it."

Do you understand the possible problem? This verse by

itself makes a case for "an eye for an eye" response, unless you read the whole of Jesus' teaching regarding the fulfillment of "the rules" or the law: "If you are slapped on one cheek, turn the other too" (v. 39). Know the principle *and* the context in which it is introduced.

Circle those statements you believe are principles:
1. Women must not work outside their homes.
2. Haircuts should reveal the entire ear.
3. The man is the head of the home.
4. Children are to live in obedience to their parents in the Lord.
5. Women should not wear pants to church.

All right, I know these are simplistic examples, but I think you get the idea. And hopefully, you have been able to separate the principles from the preferences! A coach must be conscientious about using the Word of God carefully and correctly, always basing counsel on principles.

Courageous

A coach will have courage to confront. (See Prov. 6:23; Isa. 50:4; Ezek. 3:19.)

Paul, in his letter to the Thessalonians, is counseling regarding believers who are lazy. But after the exhortation to get to work he gives direction on how to help and exhort others. This characteristic does require courage, but perhaps requires more wisdom than anything else.

Confrontation is sometimes made in anger: "It is about time someone let you have it! And I have decided that I will be that person!" But it takes special courage and wisdom, with a non-judgmental attitude, to help the woman in need to identify the root problem. It takes courage and self-control to guide if warning and confrontation is the Lord's leading.

Careful

A coach is careful to realize personal limitations. (See Jas. 3:17.)

There is a certain ego-building element in being asked for help or counsel. And there is a tendency to respond to questions with a kind of heady authority as if we are the fount of all wisdom. An especially exhilarating game we play is, "Can you top this?" In other words, whatever is your problem, my own experience will show that I have survived something even more devastating! How we misuse the delicate tool of identifying by monopolizing the conversation with the hope of diverting attention from the present problem and regaling the captive audience with our own story.

Occasionally, at *least* occasionally, a credible coach will have to admit that the situation is baffling and needs to be referred to someone more qualified to help. Understanding your personal limitations can, at times like this one, improve your effectiveness.

A good friend of mine who is a fine speaker decided it was time to have a brochure printed. It was her hope that this would clarify what exactly she "did" for a living. She began to list various areas of interest and areas in which she felt qualified to speak (she is also a gifted counselor) and was completely chagrined! Not even the Bionic Woman could be an expert in all of those assorted fields! Realizing that her effectiveness would be impaired by trying to speak to too many areas, she wisely and prayerfully limited her expertise.

Often our coaching can simply amount to guiding another through a concordance—either before, with or after a counseling session. Do not hesitate to reveal your inadequacy and affirm the adequacy of Jesus Christ.

In all practicality, it is a good idea to become acquainted with resources in your church and community for problem solving. As you assume leadership in your service, make a list or resource file to which you can refer as the need arises. Check these resources for yourself, making certain that you can endorse the principles on which the service is built.

Clear and Simple

Be able to clarify and simplify. (See Exod. 18:19; Ps. 55:14; Prov. 15:19.)

Listen attentively, then be the coach who will help to clarify rather than confuse with complicated counseling. Here are some steps to living more simply:

1. Simply believe that *God loves you* and that love is more than "no score" in tennis! Remember that His love is simple, profound, steadying. Henrietta Mears, founder of Gospel Light Publications, was asked late in her life what she would change if she had the opportunity to begin again. Her answer was simple: "I would have believed God more."

   Take a break to look up 1 John 4:6 in *The Living Bible* and write it out right here:

   _____

   _____

   _____

2. *Live one day at a time.* Now find Matthew 6:34 in *The Living Bible* and note it:

   _____

   _____

3. *Let go of all that is wrong.* Look up James 1:21 in *The Living Bible* and memorize it:

   _____

   _____

4. *Learn to visualize solutions.* God says you have won! "It is he who makes us victorious through Jesus Christ our Lord! So, my dear brothers, since future victory is sure,

be strong and steady, always abounding in the Lord's

work, for _____

_____

_____ " (1 Cor. 15:57-58, *TLB*).

5. *Keep your eye on the ball—there is a goal.* We are surrounded by a lot of encouragers in those Hebrews 12 grandstands already. Don't look too much to *others*. Look to Jesus, the Author and Finisher!

Challenging

A coach challenges to action. (See Phil. 2:12, AMP; 2 Tim. 1:6-7).

Be a coach who has some helpful ideas to aid the woman in need to take a step toward being part of the solution herself. For instance:

- Attend church regularly.

- Read at least a portion of the Bible daily.

- Read helpful, encouraging books (suggest ones you have read).

- Listen to good cassette tapes.

- Pray with thanksgiving—it is therapeutic!

- Do one thing each day to be part of the answer—wash the kitchen floor, make a phone call, clean the garage, buy yourself an ice cream cone or, as Ziggy recommends, "Try not to faint!"

- Memorize an "old man's favorite Scripture verse": "It came to pass!"

- "Do something." Three times in Psalm 42 and 43 this same refrain is written. Write out the phrase or phrases that are the most helpful for you, right now, from Psalm 42:11 in *The Living Bible:*

_____

_____

_____

Cheerful

Be a cheerful coach. (See John 16:33, *TLB;* Col. 3:16.)

Ladies, let's all go out for cheerleader! In this era of self-styled psychologists, trainers and trainees who specialize in self-therapy, let you and me be the front-runners of a Christ-styled philosophy that says in Jesus' own words:

_____

_____ (John 16:33, *TLB*).

When a certain mother enrolled at a local college for a theology course that would help her with her Sunday School teaching, her 10-year-old son Mark inquired, "Mom, are you going out for cheerleader?"

Scriptures for Coaching Others

Need	Old Testament	New Testament
Anxiety and Worry	Psalms 43:5	Matthew 6:31-32 Philippians 4:6-7,19 1 Peter 5:7
Bereavement	Deuteronomy 31:8 Psalms 27:10 Psalms 119:50	2 Corinthians 6:10 Philippians 3:8 Matthew 5:4
Comfort	Psalms 23:4 Lamentations 3:22-23	Matthew 11:28 John 14:16,18 2 Corinthians 1:3-4 2 Thessalonians 2:16-17
Confidence (developing)	Psalms 27:3 Proverbs 14:26 Isaiah 30:15	Philippians 1:6 Philippians 4:13 Hebrews 10:35
Danger (protection from)	Psalms 23:4 Psalms 34:7,17,19 Psalms 91:1-7 Isaiah 43:2	Romans 14:8
Death	Psalms 23:4 Psalms 116:15 Lamentations 3:32-33	Romans 14:8 2 Corinthians 5:1 1 Thessalonians 5:9-10 Revelation 21:4

Need	Old Testament	New Testament
Difficulties (discipline through)		Romans 8:23 2 Corinthians 4:17 Hebrews 5:8; 12:7 Revelation 3:19
Disappointment	Psalms 43:5; 55:22	John 14:27 2 Corinthians 4:8-9
Discouragement	Joshua 1:9 Psalms 27:14; 43:5	John 14:1, 27; 16:33 1 John 5:14
Faith (to encourage)		Romans 4:3; 10:17 Ephesians 2:8-9 Hebrews 11:1,7; 12:2 James 1:3, 5-6 1 Peter 1:7
Fear	Psalms 27:1; 56:11 Proverbs 3:25 Isaiah 51:12	John 14:27 Romans 8:31 2 Timothy 1:7 1 John 4:18
Forgiveness	Psalms 32:5; 51; 103:3 Proverbs 28:13 Isaiah 1:18; 55:7	1 John 1:9 James 5:15-16
Friends and Friendliness	Proverbs 18:24	John 13:35; 15:13-14 Galatians 6:1,10

Need	Old Testament	New Testament
Growing Spiritually		Ephesians 3:17-19 Colossians 1:9-11; 3:16 1 Timothy 4:15 2 Timothy 2:15 1 Peter 2:2 2 Peter 1:5-8; 3:18
Loneliness	Psalms 23; 27:10 Isaiah 40:31	Matthew 28:20 Hebrews 13:5
Love (God's)		John 15:9 Romans 5:8; 8:38-39 1 John 3:1
Obedience	1 Samuel 15:22 Psalms 111:10; 119:2	Matthew 6:24 John 14:15; 14:21 1 John 3:22
Persecution		Matthew 5:10-11,22 Acts 5:41 Romans 8:17 2 Timothy 3:12 1 Peter 2:20
Return of Christ		Acts 1:11 1 Thessalonians 4:16-18 Titus 2:13 1 John 3:2-3

Need	Old Testament	New Testament
Sickness	Psalms 41:3; 103:3	Matthew 4:23 John 11:4 James 5:15-16
Suffering		Romans 8:18 2 Corinthians 1:5 Philippians 1:29; 3:10 2 Timothy 2:12 1 Peter 2:19; 4:12-13,16; 5:10
Temptation		1 Corinthians 10:12-13 Hebrews 2:18 James 1:2-3,12,14 1 Peter 1:6 2 Peter 2:9
Victory	2 Chronicles 32:8	Romans 8:37 1 Corinthians 15:57 2 Corinthians 2:14 1 John 5:4 Revelation 3:5, 21:7

RUN YOUR RACE TO WIN!

Bev had her ticket to go to Boston for the marathon. Ann Kiemel lived in Boston and Bev had been inspired by reading all of Ann's books and decided to call her.

"Hi, Ann. I'm Bev. I just wrote you recently." After talking for some time they agreed to have lunch together the day after Bev finished the marathon.

In Ann's book, *I'm Running to Win,* these words are recorded:

"lunch today with Bev Wenshau.
she came from Minneapolis with her family to run the
    Boston marathon yesterday.
she'd written ahead, hoping to meet me
    . . . had read all my books.
suddenly, over lunch, she said . . .
'ann, you could run a' marathon, you're lean
    . . . and disciplined,
you could.'
    i looked at this young woman . . . just my age . . .
    a hero to me.
and at that moment, today, in the parker house hotel,
downtown boston, the dream was really born.
to be a runner . . . to go for broke . . . not to quit.
God helping me.
    i wonder what this really means?
    i wonder."[5]

Bev and Ann became fast friends. In fact, you will see Bev's picture in the book. Along with being a source of encouragement, she paced Ann several months later around the Sea of Galilee when Ann took a group of Boston's children to the Holy Land.

It was April 1980, and Ann was one of several women speaking in Washington, D.C. As she stepped to the microphone to speak, she seemed unsteady on her feet. "I still have bandages on my feet!" she explained. "But I finished the Boston marathon."

no one can really understand what it costs or means to
    be faithful . . .
unless he has tried to do that.
the people on the periphery, cheering the winners,
really have no comprehension of what it meant
to be out there running those miles.
they thought it looked great, and they were
impressed with people who could . . .
but they couldn't know inside what it really feels like
to put yourself on the line . . . to compete . . .
to feel the pressure and the strain and the
throb in your whole body.
i think it's the same as being true with Jesus.
unless one has really tried to be faithful . . .
really paid some price for faithfulness . . .
one doesn't understand the cost or the great
reward . . . the pain and the great joy.[6]

Is God asking you to be an athlete? If so, can you eventually picture yourself coaching other athletes? Whatever game plan God has for you, be assured that it will be hard fought at times but always exciting. Remember your vow to go for the gold and your rewards will be many. Also watch as God draws near and puts teammates in your life that will benefit from your companionship as well as provide marvelous opportunity to glorify Him.

"In a race, everyone runs but only one person gets first prize. So run your race to win" (1 Cor. 9:24, *TLB*).

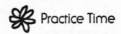 Practice Time

Sarah　　　　　　　Eve　　　　　　　Naomi
　　Rebekah　　　　　　　Martha　　　　　Esther

1. Consider each of these biblical women, one at a time.
2. Identify a crisis in each life.
3. What are some scriptural principles that can be applied to each woman's experience?
4. List three or four action points that each woman took, either during or after the crisis, that is part of the solution.
5. Can you make some alternative suggestions for more positive results?

Now come up with some variations on this exercise. Look at the lives and dilemmas of women in history and literature, some great and lesser-known Christians, and neighbors and friends. Practice being an incognito people-helper.

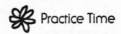 The Games People Play

Here are a few situations for you to consider. Using some scriptural principles, consider how you might help.

1. After an afternoon on the tennis court, Millie sank into a lounge chair. She was glad that Joan had agreed to join her because she needed to talk. Just the day before the pastor had challenged the congregation to think seriously about having regular family devotions in their homes. *She* had wanted to do this very thing for ages, but Roger continually ignored the suggestion. "Joan," she asked, "doesn't the Bible say that my husband is the spiritual head of our home? Isn't Roger the leader for activities such as these? What am I supposed to do if he doesn't assume his responsibility?"

2. John hurried home with *another great idea* to share with Jean! This one would work—he just *knew* it! "Jean, a good friend of mine called today with a deal that will really help us get back on our feet. There is an athletic club that

is for sale and I have been invited to go in on the deal by investing with three other guys!"

Jean sighed. There had been other financial risks, and so far, none had done them any good! Last year's scheme *had* failed and they were further than ever in debt. It had become a hardship on their family as well as on their relationship.

Based on Ephesians 5:22, is Jean required to keep quiet and just enjoy the hot tub she and John are sitting in? How can you help?

3. Betty and George's three children are now in junior and senior high school. Each of them, two boys and a girl, is involved in sports. Betty is pleased that they are doing so well in something wholesome and healthy! But it does have its complications—Betty is the chauffeur, cook, cheerleader and all-around water girl for the whole family. And even though he is an energetic husband, George has suffered some financial reverses. Recently he suggested that Betty go back to the job she left when the children started arriving 16 years ago. Though some have said that it is more important to be at home when children are small, Betty feels she needs to be available during the "teen years" as well. Help her with her priorities, will you?

4. It was more than simply a surprise, it was a shock to all the women when Carol signed her name right there with all the others for the Church League Volleyball team. Everyone knew that Carol had told her husband to leave and was now seeing another man. They also knew the children were sent off to Grandma's every so often so Carol's social life wouldn't be inhibited. Should she be allowed to join the volleyball team, just as naturally as if there were not "the other life" at all? And if not, who should be the one to tell her?

Is it now time for you to share your own crises with some good friends? What can you do to help each other?

❀ Bodily Exercise Is All Right—Part 1

Take your time and do this set of exercises three times a day—or more if you like! Also read 1 Timothy 4:7 in *The Living Bible* before you begin.

1. Stand straight. Pull in and up from your waist so that you feel taller. Pull in your stomach—harder—and count slowly to 10.

2. Relax and tighten your muscles in the buttocks—harder—and count slowly to 10.

3. Relax, then tighten the leg muscles of your right thigh—harder—and count slowly to 10. Do the same with your left thigh.

4. Clasp your hands at the back of your neck, keeping elbows out to the side. Press your head back but resist with your folded arms. Count slowly to 10.

5. With both fists on your forehead, press your head forward, applying the same resistant pressure from your fists.

6. Counting slowly to 10, press the heels of your palms together—harder—then relax. Now clasp your hands across your breast with elbows out. Try to pull your hands apart while counting slowly to 10.

Soon you will be able to extend your count on each exercise and will be surprised by the new strength you've attained.

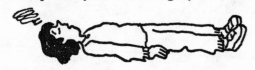

❁ Bodily Exercise Is All Right—Part 2

An avid aerobics enthusiast provided a group of less-than-exuberant Bible study members with the following list of excuses for not exercising. She then suggested that after each excuse that "fits" the women should first put a check and then an action plan. Want to try?

SAMPLE		ACTION PLAN
A. I don't have enough time.	✓	Make time between work and dinner.

1. I don't have the will power. ____
2. I don't have the energy. ____
3. I'm just not athletic enough. ____
4. I'm too tense to relax. ____
5. Equipment is too expensive. ____
6. There is no one to exercise with. ____
7. I am too old. ____
8. I am too out of shape. ____
9. It's too much trouble. ____
10. I already get enough. ____

Can you add any of your own?

11.

12.

✳ Bodily Exercise Is All Right—Part 3

Now for something a little more strenuous! All five exercises
can be done alone, with the children, with your spouse or at your
Bible study group meeting.

1. Crossover Jumps
   A. Stand erect with feet together and hands on hips.
   B. Jump, moving feet out to the side into a straddle posi-
      tion.
   C. Jump again, crossing right foot over to the left.
   D. Jump back to the straddle position then jump and
      cross left foot over right. Repeat 10 times.

2. The Roll Away
   A. Lie on your back, arms on floor and out to sides,
      shoulder high, knees bent to chest.
   B. Roll hips from side to side, touching knee to floor on
      each side. Do 10 times to each side.

3. Leg Lowering
   A. Lie down on your back, arms folded under head.
   B. Raise legs together and slowly lower, keeping them
      straight.
   C. Try to take 10 counts each time you do this exercise.
      Repeat 10 times.

4. Straddle Stretch
   A. Stand astride, hands on hips.
   B. Stretch right leg out to right, bending the knee, keep-
      ing left leg straight and foot on the floor.
   C. Return to starting position before repeating on the
      other side. Repeat 10 times.

5. Windmill
   A. Stand erect, feet shoulder-width apart, hands on hips.
   B. Bend forward, touch right hand to left foot, and *with-
      out* coming to a standing position, touch left hand to
      right foot. Repeat 10 times.

Four Steps to Spiritual Fitness

1. Eat well
   Balance intake with output!
   > Jeremiah 15:16
   > Matthew 4:4
   > 1 Peter 2:2-3

2. Get plenty of rest
   This spiritual therapy relaxes you and gives confidence and poise. It helps to create a buoyant mental attitude but moreover, it provides fresh courage and motivation.
   > Psalm 37:5-8
   > Proverbs 3:5-6
   > Proverbs 16:3
   > Philippians 4:7

3. Communicate
   Pray without a break between your regular prayer time and the rest of your day.
   > Psalm 116:2
   > Psalm 118:5-6
   > Psalm 138:7

4. Exercise
   The exciting and fulfilling results in our ability to function at maximum capacity according to God's plan. Enjoy it!
   > 1 Chronicles 28:20
   > John 10:10, *AMP*[7]

What to Do with Old Sweatshirts

(When you or they are all worn out!)

1. Use those old sweatshirts you've seen in the kids' closets or found in your teenager's "under the bed space." Even consider using some of those college mementos or souvenirs from bygone vacations—whatever is fine!

2. Sew up all the openings, allowing just enough space for stuffing with fiberfill materials or old nylons. Hand sew the remaining opening after the last piece of stuffing is in place. I promise you that you've never had such a conversation piece as the one you've just created!

3. You may want to cut off the sleeves before stuffing.

4. If you lack the energy to do either, tear up those sweatshirts and use them as dust rags.

❀ What to Do with New Sweatshirts

You can make some very special sweatshirts for your family or friends by cutting colorful fabric appliques and attaching them to the sweatshirt with iron-on bonding fabrics (available in a fabric store). Then topstitch in place with your sewing machine using a heavy zig-zag stitch. I received a Daisy shirt like this as a gift and I hardly want to wear it for fear it will be ruined . . . it is so cute. Try adding your own touches by using letters for names or slogans and calico pockets on the sleeves, etc.

Look, You're a Farmer!

THE CULTIVATION OF A FARMER

> Work hard, like a farmer who gets paid well if he raises a large crop (2 Tim. 2:6, *TLB*).

"Which is best, Mrs. Hepburn, Allis-Chalmers or John Deere?"

The boys confronted me with a question I really was not prepared to answer. I had listened to their discussion from the camp's office window and figured they would soon have to seek out a qualified referee. I smiled at those two kids right off the farm, unable to leave their loyalties behind even for a week at camp. Didn't someone once say, "You can take the boy off the farm, but you can't take the farm out of the boy"? It's true.

"Well, kids, I'd like to help you, but I don't speak farm too well," I replied.

I was raised on the sidewalks of New York and other large cities, so when a farmer talks to me about walking beans, doing all sorts of things with oats, the amount of necessary rainfall and putting everything aside—even school—for harvesttime, well, it baffles me. And it fascinates me.

The Word of God speaks farm. How much it has to say about our growing up into the fullness of our God. We are pictured as both the garden and the gardener; the farmer and the soil.

Planting the Seed in Your Life

"The seed is the word of God," it says in Luke 8:11 *(NIV)*.

And in Isaiah we read that the good seed will not return void; it will accomplish all that God has planned (see Isa. 55:10-11).

Most of us have had an abundance of good seed sown in our lives. In this day of mass evangelism, small-group Bible studies, the electronic church, neighborhood ministries and Christian books by the millions, there is no excuse for not having enough seed sown in our lives to have produced an abundant harvest by this time!

How can I ever thank the Lord for grandparents on both sides of our family, whose first priority it was to sow good seed in our lives. My mother and dad also saw to it that not only were their daughters confronted with the claims of Christ at an early age, but sowing the good seed continued during their years spent at home.

You are undoubtedly reading this book because someone else has already sown good seed in your life—and it has taken root. Think about how that happened the first time. Did your grandmother take you to Sunday School where you heard the Word of God or did someone invite you to a church service where the gospel was being preached? Was it a Bible study or a Gideon Bible in a motel room that changed your life forever? Thank God for the faithfulness of sowers.

Examining Your Heart's Soil

There was a large crowd gathering around Jesus as people came from the neighboring towns to hear Him speak. Surely there were farmers listening because Jesus lost no opportunity to communicate through the use of a parable, involving a sower and the soil. Turn to Luke 8:5 and recall the story.

"A farmer went out to sow his seed." Some seed fell on the hard pathway. The birds came and ate the seed before it got past the crust and hardened topsoil. Is this ever like your own heart? Have you had so much good seed sown that the Word has long since been snatched away through carelessness or familiarity? Can you still hear the voice of God? Or has your heart crusted over through years and years of church attendance without the Word taking root? It seems that the Pharisees listening to Jesus that day had already closed their minds to His teaching.

Dr. Lloyd John Ogilvie, in his book, *The Autobiography of God,* declares that customs, traditions and political beliefs can make Pharisees out of church members. When we hear a truth that "we do not live out, we block our sensitivity to hear further truth . . . . The greatest single cause of impaired hearing of fresh truth is the refusal to live what we already know."[1]

"The shallow, rocky soil represents the heart of man who hears the message and receives it with real joy, but he doesn't have much depth in his life, and the seeds don't root very deeply, and after a while when trouble comes, or persecution begins because of his beliefs, his enthusiasm fades, and he drops out" (Matt. 13:20-21, *NIV*).

Dr. Ogilvie also states that "bedrock is covered over with a thin layer of soil. The seed is lodged in this soil and takes root. But the roots quickly reach the impenetrable rock. Because the roots are not allowed to grow deeply and are denied the replenishment of depth nourishment, the surface plant withers in the sun. It cannot sustain its initial growth. What does this have to say about our hearing and our hearts?

Remember that the heart is the inner core of intellect, emotion and will. If one aspect of our hearts is penetrated to the exclusion of the rest, our hearing will be faulty. We will know immediate growth, but no lasting maturity."[2]

Dr. Ogilvie goes on to say that there are three kinds of Christians:

1. *The Emotional Christian*—beginning with great enthusiasm, but easily thrown off balance;

2. *The Intellectual Christian*—has not allowed Christ to deal with emotions and attitudes;

3. *The Volitional Christian*—perhaps intellectually sound and emotionally free but withered if he refuses to do God's will in the painful areas of obedience.[3]

Have you known at least one time in your life when you felt like you were shallow soil?

Thorny ground Christians are those whose hearts are crowded out and the good seed is choked, therefore denying the possibility of fruit. "He does less and less for God," *The Living Bible* says in Matthew 13:22. There are just too many thorns taking up space.

"When is a heart overcrowded? When is the good seed unable to grow because the resources of thought, energy, creativity and time are depleted on secondary loyalty to the thorns? If there is no time for listening to God in Bible study and prolonged meditation, we are too busy. When we are too distracted by duties and responsibilities to grow as persons . . . we are dangerously close to missing the reason we were born."[4]

Hurray for the good soil—the hearing heart! "The good ground represents the heart of a man who listens to the message and understands it and goes out and brings thirty, sixty, or even a hundred others into the Kingdom" (Matt. 13:23, *NIV*).

The chief characteristic of the good soil, the productive plot and the victory garden is its receptivity to the seed. Luke 8:15 *(NIV)* tells us that the good soil "stands for those with a noble and good heart, who hear the word, retain it, and by persevering produce a crop."

The difference between these kinds of soils is solely in their receptivity to the seed. Over that we have only our free will to consider! Choose to receive the Word of God, to obey it and to allow God to make it produce!

Cultivating the Shoots

"May your roots go down deep into the soil of God's marvelous love" (Eph. 3:17, *TLB*). If the life of Christ has found lodging in your heart, by receiving the seed of His Word, then you must cooperate with the elements to cultivate that new, struggling shoot. Growth is the only evidence of life, it is said, and when we are born into the Kingdom, naturally we begin to grow in faith and understanding, in love for Christ and others, in influence for Jesus and in production of fruit.

Try as we will, we cannot make ourselves grow! It is "only God who makes things grow" (see 1 Cor. 3:7). But we *can* and *must* respond to the elements of His love and care—the showers and the sunshine—to grow up. Reading and heeding His Word, and prayer with service, are tools of cultivation in your life. But here is another method that might strike a responsive note.

"Do you want a change in your life? All it takes is 15 minutes a day." This is the title and lead-in sentence to an article I read some time ago. Let me quote from it:

> What's the biggest dream of your life? How important is it? How much would you give up to make it happen? Here is an astoundingly true fact: You can do just about anything you want to do if you spend just 15 minutes a day at it.
>
> In three years you can become an expert on any subject you care to study—Chinese art, computer programming, cooking, bricklaying, gardening—if you work at it 15 minutes a day.
>
> In a year or less you could—
> * read the entire Bible
> * plant and keep up a small garden
> * become physically fit
> * learn to play a musical instrument
> * paint a house
> * learn a foreign language
> * write a book (the list is limitless).
>
> My first project was to tackle a badly neglected flower garden which was choked with weeds. Every time I looked out the dining room window, I fretted, because I thought I had no time whatsoever to try to redeem that impossible garden.
>
> Then I learned how many weeds I could pull in 15 minutes! It took just one week, snatching a quarter hour here, another there, to get that flower border tidy and ready for new transplants.
>
> The beauty of 15 minutes a day is that it helps me to stop postponing those things I really want or need to do and get them under way. It halts procrastination and banishes discouragement.[5]

The writer of the article, Charlotte Hale Allen, reports that women she interviewed suggest these 15-minute package projects: help a child tidy a room, make a beautiful dessert, take a short walk, straighten a wardrobe closet, read a chapter in a book, take a bubble bath, phone an older person, listen to God, write a note, do something special for a family member.

Be a farmer who cultivates a productive life in Christ and accepts each day—with all its quarter hours—as a gift from God. Cultivate a thankful heart and count your blessings!

Weeding the Plot

"When the wheat sprouted and formed heads, then the weeds also appeared" (Matt. 13:26, *NIV*). Weeds sap strength from the soil. Weeds also demand nourishment and get it from the food for the growing plant. Weeds are worthless.

Weeding is necessary to keep out those things which would sap the energy and nourishment necessary for the growth of the good seedling. Weeding will keep foreign plants from taking hold and choking out the life of the fruitful growth.

Weeding is also your part. "Get rid of all that is wrong in your life," James 1:21 *(TLB)* states too clearly for comfort! We are responsible to weed out the wrongs in our lives.

If you promise not to tell my musician husband, I will "sing" a little song that I learned when I was about five—along with motions that you are going to have to picture, especially the bunny part!

Root them out, get them gone
All the little bunnies in the field of corn
Envy, jealous, malice and pride,
All if allowed in my heart would abide!

There are lists of weeds in Scripture and this one comes from Galatians 5:19-21. In the audacious paraphrase of *The Living Bible,* this list comes just a little too close to my garden. What about your own? "But when you follow your own wrong inclinations your lives will produce these evil results: impure thoughts, eagerness for lustful pleasure, idolatry, spiritism (that is, encouraging the activity of demons), hatred and fighting, jealousy and anger, constant effort to get the best for yourself, complaints and criticisms, the feeling that everyone else is wrong except those in your own little group—and there will be wrong doctrine, envy, murder, drunkenness, wild parties, and all that sort of thing. Let me tell you again as I have before, that anyone living that sort of life will not inherit the kingdom of God."

Just in case you cannot find any of these weeds that have ever sprouted in your life, take a magnifying glass to Ephesians 4:25-29 or Colossians 3:5-9.

But in trying her best to weed consistently and thoroughly the farmer must avoid two things:

First, never, never, never think you can coexist with that spiritual-energy-sapping weed. It will do you in every time! Soon even the most innocuous weed will spurt growth and cut off the sun and showers from the growing plant. With the direct access to sunlight cut off, the plant will soon forget that maturity unto fruitbearing was that for which the seed was first sown. Read the Word.

Second, do not let your influence as a leader be marred by the presence of pettiness, envy, malice or pride. Do agree with God that these attitudes are in fact sin and all get weeded out. Since the weeds have no attachment to the vine or branches, it ought not to hurt to remove them. Ponder that a bit, before we move to the next step in the cultivation of a farmer, the pruning.

There's one thing I'd like to ask You, Lord.
  It has puzzled me often;
  Why do weeds grow easier than flowers?
I see it right before my eyes:
  I sow flowers and produce weeds.
  I sow grass and raise crabgrass;
my frail plants are choked by luscious dandelions.
Now I have no personal animosity against dandelions,
  Master.
  They are bright, cheerful flowers.
  Sensible too,
  for they shut up at night,
  which is more than many people do.
But why should dandelions that I don't plant
  thrive better than the flowers I protect?
How is it that from a packet of choice seeds all

I get is chickweed?
If it were only a question of flowers and weeds
    it would be strange enough,
    but the tendency goes further and
    deeper.
    I find it within my own being,
    a downward pull,
    a gravitation to a lower level.
It is a daily fight to keep the standard high,
    to bring forth flowers instead of weeds,
    good instead of evil
    in my life, character and service.
Lord, is it a law in your moral world,
    as well as in your natural world,
    that the more valuable the product
    the harder it is to produce?[6]

Pruning By a Loving Gardener

At last we have come to God's part. Pruning is often painful but productive, and is the work of the Gardener. "He cuts off every branch in me that bears no fruit, while every branch that does bear fruit he trims clean so that it will be even more fruitful. You are already clean because of the word I have spoken to you" (John 15:2-3, *NIV*).

Please don't confuse the weeding and the pruning processes as some do when they ask, "Why is God doing this to me? Why is God letting this happen in my life?"

Some of the things that are hurting us are simply a result of our own sin. We are responsible to see that weeds are removed by our choice and confession. The Lord will not sow sin in your life so that you can experience the pain of pruning. Negative and confusing attitudes or actions are not sown into your leadership experiences by the Gardener of your heart! Those are weeds. As you take another look at John 15, note that only grown-up, mature, fruitbearing branches are able to be pruned.

We were driving through the Fresno Valley of California last fall when we saw acre upon acre of grape stumps. The vine-dressers had recently gone up and down the rows, lopping off those vines that had been dragging to the ground with succulent bunches of grapes hardly any time before. It took a while for those newly planted grapevines to grow to that fruitbearing stage. Care and training are required before the farmer prunes "back for greater strength and usefulness" (John 15:3, *TLB*). His harvest is at stake and he knows what he is doing.

Is God allowing circumstances, associations and testing to enter your life according to His timing, to increase your strength?

Joni Eareckson Tada has experienced pruning. In the most recent movie of her life, in which she testifies to the sustaining power of God as she learned to adapt to being a quadraplegic, Joni is a powerful witness. She is able to say that were she to have to trade what God has come to mean to her through the "tragedy" of losing the use of her limbs, for the ability to become upright and independent of her wheelchair, she would not be able to do it. For greater strength and usefulness, Joni has been pruned back.

Today Joni has a ministry in Southern California for handicapped persons. There is no way to count the lives that have been influenced to Christ or have been encouraged to trust God through Joni's spiritual fruitbearing. She recognizes that her life is probably far more useful to the Lord than it ever could have been had she been allowed to pursue the pattern of the "normal" young American girl.

Think about that which pricks your pride—those thorns that are so troublesome to you. Are the things which are hurting you merely weeds? Or are they part of God's pruning in your life because you have been forgiven up-to-date of all known sin?

Pruning is an indication of God's loving care, to make you into His useful, productive person. The Lord Jesus cares about you and your service to Him. He has placed inestimable value upon you, and it is His plan that you should "(attain) the whole measure of the fullness of Christ" (Eph. 4:13, *NIV*).

Dr. E. Stanley Jones has written these words: "A Christian yielded to God and His work within uses his pains, sets them to music, makes them sing. Every jolt only jolts the glory out. Every kick only kicks him forward. Even if he stumbles, he stumbles forward. He is like the apple trees which had especially fine apples on them. When asked the reason, the owner pointed to the slashes on the trunk of the tree, saying, 'For some reason the trees bear better fruit when slashed and wounded in this way. So we slash them into added fruitfulness.'"[7]

Grow up so that God can begin to really shape your life. Allow Him to prune you through disciplines in your leadership. J.B. Phillips has translated Hebrews 12:11 like this: "But God corrects us all our days for our own benefit, to teach us his holiness. Now obviously no 'chastening' seems pleasant at the time: it is in fact most unpleasant. Yet when it is all over we can see that it has quietly produced the fruit of real goodness in the characters of those who have accepted it in the right spirit."

Now take a fresh grip on life.

Harvesting Your Fruit with Joy

In the fullness of His timing, fruit is produced. Depend upon it! Let your concentration be upon the abiding. "If [anyone] remains in me and I in him, he will bear much fruit" (John 15:5, *NIV*). We have been chosen to produce fruit.

To me, a pathetic part of Scripture is Isaiah 5:1-6 *(NIV)*:

I will sing for the one I love
    a song about his vineyard:
My loved one had a vineyard
    on a fertile hillside.
He dug it up and cleared it of stones,
    and planted it with the choicest vines.
He built a watchtower in it
    and cut out a winepress as well.
Then he looked for a crop of good grapes,
    but it yielded only bad fruit.
"Now you dwellers in Jerusalem
    and men of Judah,
judge between me and my
    vineyard.
What more could have been done
    for my vineyard
    than I have done for it?

When I looked for good grapes,
    why did it yield only bad?
Now I will tell you
    what I am going to do
    to my
    vineyard.
I will take away its hedge,
    and it will be destroyed;
I will break down its wall,
    and it will be trampled.
I will make it a wasteland,
    neither pruned nor cultivated,
and briers and thorns will grow
    there.
I will command the clouds
    not to rain on it."

Do you picture the Saviour laboring to provide the best possible conditions for growing and reaping a harvest of fine fruit? Can you hear the pathos when no crop is realized, "What more could have been done?"

Is it too harsh to suggest that God ought to be able to see more fruit from His farmers' lives—from our ministries? The Bible suggests that there are several kinds of fruit that the Christian can and should be producing. Here are just a few:

❁ Spiritual Fruit Fit for Harvesting

1. Philippians 1:11: _____

_____

2. Colossians 1:10: _____

_____

3. Galatians 5:22-23: _____

_____

4. Hebrews 13:15: _____

_____

We are identified by the fruit we bear! What commends a certain apple tree to you? The sight of big red apples on its branches! I sure wish I had the nerve to say to some women I meet what was said by someone braver than I from a pulpit one day: I would believe in your Redeemer if you looked more redeemed!

I guess I have always envied a bit those farmers' wives who have fresh vegetables on their table at every meal, their freezers full before Thanksgiving and that old-fashioned fruit cellar lined with glass jars of tomatoes, pickles and peaches. But I think I am like the little boy who, when asked what he wanted to be when he grew up, replied, "Either a returned veteran, a retired missionary or a plantation owner." I would like to be a farmer after the harvest . . . if only there was some way to shortcut the hard work involved!

One of the happy by-products of serving Christ as a farmer is the opportunity to enjoy the firstfruits. Who do you think is receiving the maximum benefit from this book? *Me!* Of course. God is making me dig in, think through, write out and make certain of all that you are reading. The teacher is the best taught, the leader is most thoroughly blessed, the reward is the greatest for the one who has invested the most time and effort.

As a matter of fact, unless *you* are getting fed, enriched and nourished through your study and preparation, you will not be effective in feeding others.

Be a farmer who is the first to enjoy the fruit of your labor in leadership.

SERVANT-FARMING

There are four basic activities servant-farmers involve themselves in to make their ministries significant, successful and glorifying to God. Once you have cultivated your own life as a farmer, you'll want to involve yourself in the following activities:

Plowing

I believe there are two reasons why a farmer plows: First, to turn over the soil that has not been used for planting recently and to break up the crust; Second, to plow back into the ground those stems and roots left there after the harvest has been gathered.

"Break up your unplowed ground and do not sow among thorns" (Jer. 4:3, *NIV*). A farmer realizes that the fallow, crusted ground must be turned over. It must be prepared. In your ministry you must be careful to prepare the soil before you sow seed willy-nilly among thorns. Before you even consider launching into a new ministry, prepare the area with the hardest and most effective work you can do—prayer.

Or perhaps, after a particularly rich time of harvest, you might pull back and plow under with prayer before a new planting is made. The Lord will honor your efforts.

A farmer's wife set to work clearing some rocky, overgrown soil "outback." She worked hard to prepare it for planting because she had a special garden in mind. It had possibilities—but what a job it turned out to be!

The preacher passed by one day as the lady was standing in the midst of her now-productive garden, pleasuring it. The preacher commented, in spiritual tones, "What a wonderful garden God has given you. You must be very thankful."

The lady reflected, then replied, "Yes, but you should've seen it when God had it alone!"

Investing

Any farmer worth his salt invests; he won't just look out the farmhouse window, surveying endless acreage and decide to go the route of least effort. *There's so much risk involved. What would happen if a hailstorm were to blow across my land come midsummer? The safe way is simply to make the smallest possible investment—just in case. I don't think I'll plant too much this year.*

If you would reap a harvest, you will have to invest the most and the best that you can.

This think-small attitude usually strikes a church's women's ministry program about springtime. It is worse than spring fever! You have worked hard all fall and winter, planned meetings, recruited "farmhands" to be on kitchen committees, served at receptions and made certain the nursery workers' roster was filled for both services. Summer cannot come soon enough for you, and as you think about the fall and the salad supper to get everybody rallied again, you almost yield to temptation. *Maybe the women should not get so involved next year. It's so much trouble. If the church cuts the missions budget, we won't have to work so hard. Let's cut down the number of teachers' meetings, let's leave out—let's pare down—let's not go out on a limb.*

Scripture tells us that whatever we sow we will reap. "And let us not get tired of doing what is right, for after a while we will reap a harvest of blessing if we don't get discouraged and give up" (Gal. 6:9, *TLB*).

It was the best potato crop anyone could remember. There were mountains of potatoes! The legend says that all the villagers had potatoes on their tables every day. Baked, boiled, mashed—the biggest and best. They ate them raw, peeled or plain. They saved the scrubby ones for seeding and enjoyed the prize potatoes.

A few years passed and the strangest thing happened to the potato crop—it shrunk! No longer did they have big meaty, snow-white potatoes. They had to be content with little, brown, bullet-size spuds. Why? Because they had sowed the leftovers for too long. If they wanted good, big potatoes, they were going to have to sow some of the good, big potatoes.

It is not quite the same in your ministry, for God graciously multiplies and magnifies our efforts. But still we must invest our best—in faith—that He will increase it. Be a woman who spares nothing and holds back nothing, and you will enjoy the maximum harvest for your labors.

Be Careful What You Sow

As we sow, so we must reap,
Both the bitter, and the sweet;
While we tread this earthly road,
Each must bear a heavy load;
One small deed, of sin or strife,
May mar or wreck an entire life.
Then be careful what you sow,
Very careful how you sow.

Oh! the joy, and oh! the gain,
Of one seed sown in His name;
Then for the Master, sweetly sow,
While you journey here below;
And keep your lamp, all burning bright,
It will scatter sin's dark night.
Then be careful what you sow,
Very careful how you sow.

For the Lord's laid up in store,
E'en an hundredfold or more;
For every evil seed you sow,
'Twill surely bring a crop of woe;
And every word, or thought, or deed,
Is a sweet or bitter seed.
Thus be careful what you sow,
Very careful how you sow.

Oh, the sorrow and the pain,
Of our seed that's sown in vain;
It will bring no end of woe,
While you're here and where you go.
Death's dark night it will increase,
And God's love will surely cease.
Then be careful! what you sow,
Very careful how you sow.[8]

Cooperating with Conditions

A farmer doesn't sow in autumn nor plow in the dead of winter. A farmer reads the almanac and plans his year's work. He is adaptable when adjustments must be made for unexpected weather changes. Be a wise and careful farmer. Plan and cooperate with God. "Peacemakers who sow in peace raise a harvest of righteousness" (Jas. 3:18, *NIV*).

Paul reminded the Corinthians that no farmer is more important than another, and cooperation is the key to getting the job done. "My work was to plant the seed in your hearts . . . the person who does the planting or watering isn't very important, but God is important because he is the one who makes things grow" (1 Cor. 3:6-7, *TLB*).

We are God's co-workers; cooperate with Him.

Expecting a Harvest

By far the most important characteristic of a farmer is optimism. Picture a gardener, kneeling in the dirt, seeds all selected, trowel and watering can at hand. With every little hole dug she thinks, *It'll never grow. I've never had any luck with plants. It's impossible. The seeds don't look right. It's probably too sunny here—or too shady—or the neighbor's dog will choose this spot to bury his bone.*

On a larger scale, can a farmer afford to expect disaster? Faith and risk go together, just as surely as faith and work. Remember Psalm 42:11 *(TLB)*, "Expect God to act!"

• • •

It was touch-and-go this last month for a small committee of women in San Jose, California. The chairwoman for the special interdenominational prayer breakfast had invested weeks in planning and prayer. The restaurant was reserved, the menu checked, the finances arranged, tickets printed, and speakers and musicians contacted. Several prayer times had focused on this one event. With just two weeks to go, only a handful of tickets had been sold. The chairwoman called her friend Audrey in desperation.

"Audrey, when do we decide that this has gone far enough? It just won't work. It is only good business to face our limitations; we should cancel if we don't have at least 200 reservations by this weekend."

Audrey would have no part of such negativism. To believe that the Lord was planning the direction for the breakfast and had specific purposes for this meeting, required a belief that prayer would have an effect. God would act! And He did! Never have I seen the San Jose women so excited—well over 300 men and women came. The Lord met us there. Audrey believed that it was God's way to do "exceeding abundantly above all that we could ask or think." Either prayer and trust in God are the added dimensions in our Christian lives and ministries or they are not.

Are you a servant-leader who expects the blessing of God on your ministry, your time, your abilities and your planning? Be a farmer who cooperates with the conditions, invests only your best and trusts God for the increase!

🌸 Work Hard, Like a Farmer

1. A farmer plows.
   Jeremiah 4:3: _____

   _____

2. A farmer invests.
   Matthew 25:16,21: _____

   _____

   _____

   _____

   2 Corinthians 9:6: _____

   _____

3. A farmer cooperates with conditions.

   1 Corinthians 3:5-9: _____

   _____

   _____

   _____

4. A farmer expects a harvest.
   Galatians 6:7-9: _____

   _____

   _____

Hoeing

It's just the day for it, Lord!
What a delightful sensation when the needs of the moment
Coincide with my inward urge to do a job!
Those jaunty tufts of grass mock me
with their exuberance
for they're growing in the wrong place,
having promoted themselves to the flower beds.
"Out with you," I say, as I lop their heads off,
"Away with you," as I dig their roots loose.
What a battle in a few square yards of garden!
No wonder the jungle can silently and remorselessly
encroach on pillared cities,
engulfing them in rolling green waves,
strangling them to death.
While I work, I think.
My thoughts circle around the weeds that fester and grow in the
human heart.
All right, I admit it Lord, in *my* heart.
Irritations, resentments, self-centeredness, envy . . .
what ugly things grow in the garden of my heart,
just as persistent,
just as perennial
as weeds in the flower beds.
"Out with them," I say . . .
but I don't know how to root them out.
Only you can do that, Master.
You must be my divine Gardener with your pruning
knife and hoe.[9]

Sample Devotional Page for Agenda Cover

Here are some Scripture resources for a prayer time at your committee meeting:

"Why, we're just God's servants, each of us with certain special abilities, and with our help you believed. My work was to plant the seed in your hearts, and Apollos' work was to water it, but it was God, not we, who made the garden grow in your hearts. The person who does the planting or watering isn't very important, but God is important because he is the one who makes things grow. Apollos and I are working as a team, with the same aim, though each of us will be rewarded for his own hard work. We are only God's co-workers. You are *God's* garden, not ours; you are *God's* building, not ours" (1 Cor. 3:5-9, *TLB*).

"The seed is God's message to (women) . . . But the good soil represents honest, good-hearted people. They listen to God's words and cling to them and steadily spread them to others who also soon believe" (Luke 8:11,15, *TLB*).

"Yes, God will give you much so that you can give away much, and when we take your gifts to those who need them they will break out into thanksgiving and praise to God for your help. So, two good things happen as a result of your gifts—those in need are helped, and they overflow with thanks to God. Those you help will be glad not only because of your generous gifts to themselves and to others, but they will praise God for this proof that your deeds are as good as your doctrine" (2 Cor. 9:11-13, *TLB*).

WHAT'S COMING UP?

After you have recruited your committee, using scriptural principles, and have appointed one person to be responsible for each phase of your program, ministry or event, call a meeting of the committee. This must be a report session and not a discussion time—otherwise you will find yourself frustrated when the meeting is over and the last cup of coffee is drained. Your time will have been spent deciding on the flavor of cupcakes and the color of the invitations, rather than coordinating the decisions of the subcommittees who are to make those preliminary recommendations.

Cultivating a Successful Committee Meeting

Following is a checklist of things you should do to prepare for a committee meeting:

Secure the room or place of meeting. Clear the meeting through the church office to be sure it gets on the church calendar.

Announce to each committee member the time, date, place of meeting, either by mail or phone—or both.

Prepare and duplicate an agenda because—

- it will help you gauge your timing. One superintendent I know prepares the agenda with the time estimate for each item in the left margin.
- it sometimes negates the need for minutes, as each committee member notes on her own agenda sheet the ideas and decisions that are shared. It also improves our memories, as you'll see—

Now, Let's Dig In

Here is a sample agenda. Can you make it into a creative guide for a women's board meeting? Use the theme, "Get Up and Grow." Look up some Scripture that seems to be appropriate and use seed packets for favors, gardening tools for a table centerpiece and even fruit salads for refreshments! Clip phrases from a nursery ad, or a seed catalog, include some sketches or pictures and make it a memorable meeting!

Agenda

1. Devotions
2. Secretary's Report
3. Treasurer's Report
4. Committee Reports
   a. Program
   b. Membership
   c. Service
5. Old Business (Sample)
   a. Drapes for fellowship hall
   b. Cookbook sales
   c. Missionary project
6. New Business (Sample)
   a. Fall retreat
   b. Visit to nursing home
   c. Serving at the pastor's reception
7. Coming Events
8. Adjourn

It was a Friday afternoon and Christmas was near. Wanting to express how important the guild meeting was to which I had been invited to speak, I donned a long, red and green dress and slipped all the way to the church on the icy Minneapolis streets. The aroma of coffee cake and coffee and the scent of fresh greenery met each woman who entered the festive fellowship hall.

Those of us who were part of the program sat up front in a semicircle around a large desk. The chairwoman pounded her gavel and called this Christmas meeting to order. While we were all eyeing the calorie-laden buffet tables—and beginning to drift into that cozy after-lunch-early-afternoon euphoria common to afternoon women's meetings—the chairwoman called for the minutes!

The secretary stood, opened her book and began: "The Women's Guild Board meeting, held on such-and-such a date, did such-and-such things, including the decision to recommend to the guild-at-large the following—"

Panic! The secretary leafed through pages of minutes—all those records of monumental decisions gone by and all those laboriously worded edicts, but she couldn't find the recommendation. What could she do? With her face burning—or was it just the wavering glow of the candlelight—she dashed from the room. We sang a snatch of a Christmas carol and then the kitchen door flew open as the secretary emerged to take her place again.

Whew! How glad we were that the lost had been found—but what did it say? You won't believe this, but cross my heart and hope to die it was true! "The Board of the Women's Guild makes this recommendation—that we dispense with all business at the Christmas tea!"

The vote was taken and after it was moved, seconded and voted upon, we dispensed with the business. Minutes are necessary, but let them not be read at every meeting. Nearly 10 minutes of prime time was spent on that irrelevant piece of business.

• • •

Now, back to the reasons for preparing an agenda:
- it creates accountability. Each woman is responsible to the rest of her committee for her homework.
- it is a tangible way to emphasize the need for prayer—providing a list of things that need to be prayed for. The agenda could be printed on colored paper or stationery and have an emblem or decorative seal in the corner.

Decorate your meeting area. Use this as an opportunity to make the setting conducive to business. There is a ministry in a bowl of flowers, pretty napkins and tiny favors. Obviously, it is a signal that "you have prepared ahead of time." It tends to communicate that something very important is about to happen.

Plan refreshments. Now some people don't like "eatin'

meetins'" but simple, pretty refreshments enhance fellowship, *I* think. Ever consider sharing a recipe as part of your agenda? Since most people do not arrive together, it is my suggestion that your committee meetings be conducted around one or more tables, with the refreshments available as the women arrive.

Allow for only six or seven minutes of settling in by pouring coffee and encouraging conversation before you go to work on that agenda. Begin with a time with the Lord, led by one who has previously been asked to do so.

And never forget that there are still those women in each organization for whom *Robert's Rules of Order* will never go out of style.

Have you ever been part of a committee that weeps when the event is over? Make your committee service unforgettable; a time to build and deepen fellowship and to learn to appreciate each other's gifts and abilities. Discover that this sisterhood of believers is a serendipity of service. You will be warmly remembered if you are a committee chairwoman who makes your meetings occasions and keeps them report sessions, not discussion groups.

The country parson had this idea for a productive garden. Can you see how it could be a launching agenda for a committee meeting? Your centerpieces could be baskets of vegetables: refreshments, raw vegetables with a special dip, served with crackers.

First, plant five rows of peas—Preparedness, Promptness, Perseverance, Politeness and Prayer.

Next to them plant three rows of squash: Squash indifference, Squash gossip and Squash criticism.

Then five rows of lettuce: Let us be faithful, Let us be truthful, Let us be unselfish, Let us be loyal, Let us love one another.

And no garden is complete without turnips: Turn up for church, Turn up with a smile, Turn up with a new idea, Turn up with determination.

Sow, Hoe and Then Mow the Crop!

SOW—a good idea, a good work.

HOE—out the weeds and insects, especially the *ants*.

    c*ant*—don't get discouraged.

    w*ant*—you will want to quit and give up.

    anti—don't let anti-accomplishing thoughts take over; don't give up or be taken over by a negative point of view.

MOW—the crop, see your ideas or job through to fulfillment.[10]

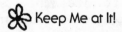 Keep Me at It!

"God, give me due respect for the abilities you have given me. Don't let me sell them short. Don't let me cheapen. Don't let me bury my talents through indecision, cowardice, or laziness. *Plant in me the necessary determination. Keep me at it.* Rouse in me the fires of dedication. *Keep me at it.* Give me the energy, strength, and will power to bring your gifts to their proper fruition. *Keep me at it.* When I falter or fall lift me up and set me back on my destined path.

Keep me at it![11]

Cultivating a Resource File

Are you the type of woman who has a place for everything? Then stop reading—this next section is for those of us with kitchen junk drawers; with dresser drawers stuffed with memorable notes, bookmarks and old programs; with glove compartments full of last week's and last year's Sunday bulletins (too pretty to toss); and last but not least, with a garage overflowing with Christmas cards, birthday cards and get-well cards from your first surgery.

Need I say more? Some of us are pack rats. I cannot remember the last time I read or saw something that I did not consider recycling either in a conversation or a craft!

At last, a system to help you get organized!

Here is a way you can create a resource file for preserving a lot of things you want to keep.

1. Assemble the following materials: manila folders as needed; 8½ × 11-inch paper; all the clippings you wish to save on any and all subjects.

2. On each 8½ × 11-inch piece of paper glue or tape the articles to be filed. Attach as many as will fit on each sheet, according to the subject or topic. Use only one side of each paper and be sure to note the source, date and author for future reference.

3. Number each 8½ × 11-inch sheet of clippings in the upper right corner consecutively. Place those pages numbered 1-25 in the first folder. As you continue to add material that you gather, prepare it the same way. The next folder will contain pages numbered 26-50; then 51-75; etc.

4. Beginning with the first page of clippings, write across the top of a 3 × 5-inch card a subject heading appropriate to the

first article on sheet 1. Under this first general topic put page 1.

That article might be more easily located if you also cross-reference it under an alternate heading. So make another 3 × 5-inch card on the alternate topic as well, also listing page 1 on it. You may need up to three cards, with three different headings for that one article.

If there are other clippings on page 1, repeat the procedure for each subject or heading on a separate 3 × 5-inch card. Follow through with all your pages of clippings, recording on the appropriate card the page number where the article is found.

Now when you have to give a two-minute motivational message, you'll go to your 3 × 5-inch card file, look under *"farmer"* or *"motivation"* or *"optimism"* and you will find just the page number you need to locate the article you want!

6. Following is a clipping that just fits. You better copy it or type it onto another piece of paper so you won't have to cut up this book—or you will never remember these instructions!

Hurrah for the Hen!

Hard work means nothing to a hen. She just keeps on digging worms and laying eggs regardless of what the business prognosticators say about the outlook for this or any other year. If the ground is hard or dry she scratches harder. If she strikes a rock, she works around it. If she gets a few more hours of daylight, she gives us a few more eggs—but she always digs up worms and turns them into hard-shelled profits as well as tender, profitable broilers. Did you ever see a pessimistic hen? Did you ever hear of one starving to death waiting for worms to dig themselves up? Did you ever hear one cackle because work was hard? Not on your life!! They save their breath for digging and their cackles for eggs. Success means digging! Are you digging?

MRS. CRAIG'S BOUNTIFUL GARDEN

Mrs. Craig was a cottage mother at the Lytton Children's Home in Sonoma County, California. Her second calling was definitely that of a farmer. Twenty-two, and sometimes even more, little boys were in her charge. They were almost the youngest group of boys in the home for 130 underprivileged boys and girls, and they ranged in age from 9 to 11.

There was no discussion, but every one of her boys knew he was expected to do his stint in the garden. Ma Craig would walk it all out near the cottage, measuring and planning the garden. Then the boys were enlisted. She enticed them with visions of buttered corn on the cob and watermelon feeds—as well as all manner of goodies to be purchased from the sale of their produce. What pride those kids took in their garden! Mulch and manure, sunshine and sweat, planting and prodding, working and weeding—it was a never-ending cycle.

One unforgettable night the boys from Oaks Cottage treated the entire home, staff and kids to a golden dinner of home-grown corn with fruit salad for dessert! You know, of course, that Ma Craig was growing a lot more than vegetables—she was growing boys!

One particular boy needed more cultivation than some of Ma's other charges. His name was Leroy Henderson and he was from the Los Angeles County Juvenile Hall.

One day a group of beautiful young people came to lead a Sunday morning Mother's Day service for the children and an invitation was given to receive Christ. This invitation was often extended, but when Leroy heard it *this* time, it seemed like God was talking to his heart in a special way.

Gleefully responding to that tiny bit of light that flooded his heart, he decided that day to follow Jesus. A personable young man spent time with Leroy, counseling, sharing and praying with him. But praying and reading the unfamiliar Bible was not going to come easily to Leroy.

He went to his cottage that evening, got down by his bed and tried to pray. Flying back and forth above his head, in that room housing 13 other boys, were everything from socks to baseballs. Finally Leroy could stand it no longer so he stood up and said,

"Listen, you guys, I'm trying to pray—so, be quiet!"

Leroy knelt again, but this time there was loud talking, hammering and pouncing even on his bed. Leroy lifted his head again and said, "Okay, you guys, I told you once I gotta pray—so *shut up!*"

Donning his football helmet for protection, he knelt again. But the kids were not about to give up that easily on their harassment.

Waiting as long as he could, Leroy Henderson jumped to his feet and yelled out for all the world to hear, "Listen you guys, that guy told me to pray and I'm going to pray if I have to kill every single one of you to do it!"

Now that's determination! It's a bit misguided, but it *is* determination, that is for sure!

I will never forget Leroy Henderson. He promised that after he made his first million dollars he would buy David and me our own church. I wonder where Leroy Henderson is now . . . .

Ma Craig planted so many seeds into the lives of her boys. Who would dare to measure the fruit produced in their lives as the years have passed from one season to the other?

Be a sower of seeds and rejoice with God at the bountiful harvest.

BE A FARMER IN YOUR OWN KITCHEN

Grow Your Own Sprouts

Growing quantities of delicious sprouts is simple enough to be child's play—and the results are good enough to eat, and great for you.

Buy alfalfa seeds at kitchen stores, health food stores, or at some markets. One ounce can yield four or five crops of delicious sprouts.

Use two tablespoons of seeds for each quart jar you start. Soak the seeds overnight; drain well and put in the jar.

Punch a few holes in the jar lid, then add the seeds.

Stretch a square doubled of a piece of nylon stocking, or cheesecloth if you like over the top of the jar, securing with a rubber band. Set the jar on its side in your kitchen cupboard.

Rinse the seeds with water twice a day; drain well after each rinsing. Just run some water gently through the nylon and pour out without removing the fabric. Shake the seeds a bit so that they don't "clump" as they begin to sprout in the jar.

The seeds will sprout in four or five days—and at this stage will almost fill the jar! If the sprouts haven't turned green before "harvesttime" set them in the sunshine for a while. Use the sprouts on salads or in sandwiches.

Prepare Potatoes

Remember the potato story and the cultivation of the tiny, scrubby ones? Let's rethink the potato and enjoy them for dinner—as a main dish, no less!

1. *Bake some good big Idahos* and serve them to your family with a variety of toppings. Try chili, taco makings, cheese and bacon, sour cream, fresh steamed vegetables, etc. This is *party fare* to be sure! Why not serve them on St. Patrick's Day?

2. *Potato skins* are finding their way to the menus in some of the best restaurants. Why not to your table? Bake the potatoes, scoop out most of the meat and treat the skins as chips for dipping. They even become a kind of nacho when cheese is melted over them before serving. Let your imagination go.

3. *Potato Casserole*

8 medium potatoes, cooked	1 envelope dry onion soup mix
¼ cup margarine or butter	½ cup sour cream
1 an cream of chicken soup	1 cup milk
1 can cream of mushroom soup	2 cups grated cheddar cheese

Combine all three soups with the margarine and heat thoroughly. Blend in sour cream, milk and half of the cheese. Alternate potatoes and soup mixture in a 2-quart casserole dish. Sprinkle the remaining cheese on top. Cover and bake at 350 degrees for 45 minutes. Remove cover and brown for 10 minutes more. Serves 8-10. A good partner to roasts and steak.

4. Ever tried to make a *potato stamp?* They're a simple alternative to stenciling. Cut a pattern from the raw half of a potato, dip into paint and stamp on to stationery. Fun for kids as well!

The Neighbor's Chickens

The story is told of a man who raised chickens. Among them was a rooster who occasionally crowed and greatly annoyed the next-door neighbor. Early one morning, disturbed and angry, the neighbor called the owner of the flock and made this complaint, "That miserable bird of yours keeps me up all night!"

"I don't understand," answered the owner. "He hardly ever crows. But if he does, it's never more than two or three times in an entire day."

The man quickly retorted, "That isn't my problem. It's not how *often* he crows that irritates me! It's not knowing when he *might* that keeps me awake!"

Many of us are like that man, aren't we? We worry about the difficulties and distressing circumstances that *could* arise tomorrow. Rather than living one day at a time and rejoicing in the Lord's sufficiency for the present, we become anxious by borrowing trouble and constantly fretting about the things we fear might happen. Someone has said that ninety percent of all the things people worry about never happen and the Lord knows all about the other 10 percent! Think about it.

Woe to the house where the hen crows louder than the rooster!

Clip and glue to cardboard after coloring with felt pens. Cover with clear contact paper and fix a 2-inch piece of magnetic tape to the back. *Voilà!* A refrigerator reminder to keep or give away!

Look, You're a Workman!

THE WORKMAN'S TOOLS

Work hard so God can say to you, "Well done." Be a good workman, one who does not need to be ashamed when God examines your work. Know what his Word says and means (2 Tim. 2:15, *TLB*).

It all takes place in a carpenter shop. The tools are having an argument and the hammer is up front, trying to call for order.

"Things need to be changed around here!" The hammer raises his voice above the din. "There are problems needing to be solved. We must get the work done, and I've thought of a solution: We must get rid of the troublemakers. As a matter of fact, we can do without the saw. The saw only makes a mess and this shop would be better off without him."

The saw hears the hammer's words about how they need to clean up and is quick to answer, "Just a minute! The hammer is the one who is always flying off the handle around here. All he does is pound, pound, driving home his point. I think we could well do without *him*."

The wrench hears the argument and as usual, opens his mouth to add fuel to the fire.

The saw retorts, "Yes, you too, wrench, have the biggest mouth around this shop and we all want you to leave!"

The wrench, when it has the chance, says, "I know I've got problems, but they are nothing compared to those of the measure. That measure has one standard and it is its own. It measures everything and everybody by itself. Couldn't we do without the measure?"

"The plane can go anytime," says the measure. "It has no depth to anything it does. It only skims the surface of the situation—it's superficial." The plane hears the measure muttering and pushes the chisel to the center of the floor before adding, "I may not be the most useful tool in this shop, but the chisel just takes pleasure in digging in. Dig, dig, dig, in every situation. Seems to delight in hurting others. Never misses an opportunity to get one more dig in."

"All right, fellas, I know I have a bit of a personality problem, but do you realize that the file is only good for one thing, too—to rub things the wrong way? We would have a little peace in the shop if it weren't for the file."

Into the shop roll a couple of nuts. "Hi fellas, what's going on?" As they hear the argument they are quick to join in with, "Go on and argue if you want to, but remember that we are what holds things together around here. We may only be a couple of nuts, but you couldn't do without us!"

Quiet up until now, the level finally speaks. "Actually, my good brothers, I guess I'm the only one who is really on the level in this shop. Perhaps someday you'll understand and appreciate my transparent dependability."

What a commotion! Suddenly the door swings open and a pile of wood lumbers into the shop and, when it lays itself in a pile on the floor, it says, "Go ahead, go to work on us. We know that every time we come in here you have a different idea about what we ought to be. You seem to think that we need to be made over—so go to it." Discouraged, the wood just lays there.

Clump, clump, clump—in comes the sawhorse with a sigh and says, "At last the burden-bearer in this shop has arrived. Everybody, see these broad shoulders? Well, they were made to bear the burdens of all the rest of you, I guess." There was more than a note of self-pity in the tones of the sawhorse, and it prompted all kinds of responses from the rest of the tools.

They don't even stop for long when the door opens and the Carpenter of Nazareth Himself walks into the shop. There seems to be a holy hush however, when He puts on His work apron and sits at the bench, going about His task. First He picks up one tool, and then another, humming as He works. This goes on all day long and the tools find themselves being used.

At the end of the day, as the sun casts a warm glow on the work of the Carpenter, the tools begin to wonder what it was they were being used to build. The hammer, with awe, announces to the others as he looks up toward the sky, "Why, we've been used to build a cathedral; a temple for the living God!"

Every accusation which the tools made about one another was absolutely true. Yet, during the construction, not one was used where another would have done as well. Not one was indispensable. As they ponder the work, one of them, perhaps the hammer—murmurs, "Brethren, I perceive that we are laborers together with God." (See 1 Cor. 3:9.)

Working together is easier to imagine than to execute. The "tools" tend to be abrasive and sharp, even self-seeking. As we consider 2 Timothy 2:15 and as it relates to our service and leadership, perhaps this chapter could be considered our blueprint for learning to help other women lay a solid foundation in their lives.

A Wise Woman Is a Builder

I once heard Lila Trotman, the widow of Dawson Trotman, who founded the Navigator Movement, tell the story about how God had almost mystically allowed her husband to know that he was soon going to heaven. They were seated together by a lake and Dawson took the time to carefully tell her about how God had raised up the Navigator movement during the Second World War, about its workings and the plans for the future of the organization.

He also mentioned some immediate leadership responsibilities that might fall on her shoulders.

Two weeks later Dawson drowned, while trying to save another, in that same lake. Over and over again it sobered Lila to realize how God had prepared Dawson in order that her husband could prepare her.

Their home had always been the central location for fellowship and training. People were always around her table—because of their growing family and their burgeoning ministry. But suddenly she had to come to grips with the management of their home *and* the responsibility of the ministry; she had to work with people without her husband's support, to step into situations that she didn't feel suited to, and at the same time handle her grief. How could she do it?

One of the disciplines she began was to read one specific chapter in the Bible seven times a day! Of course she had learned 1 Corinthians 13 by heart—but she read it until the desire for love engulfed and possessed her.

But there were moments of tension as the adjustments in the organization were made. Submitting herself to the shaping and molding of God in her own life, she was able to pray a simple, life-controlling prayer: "Lord, let me never enter a life except to build!"

Except to build.

Do you affirm that this is a foundation prayer in the life of the Godly woman workman?

> God, in his kindness, has taught me how to be an expert builder. I have laid the foundation and Apollos has built on it. But he who builds on the foundation must be very careful. And no one can ever lay any other real foundation than that one we already have—Jesus Christ. But there are various kinds of materials that can be used to build on that foundation. Some use gold and silver and jewels; and some build with sticks, and hay, or even straw! There is going to come a time of testing at Christ's Judgment Day to see what kind of material each builder has used. Everyone's work will be put through the fire so that all can see whether or not it keeps its value, and what was really accomplished (1 Cor. 3:10-13, *TLB*).

Are You a Builder?

Take a few minutes away from your work and think a bit about these things:

- Think about at least three people whose lives you have entered in the last week.
- Think about the ways in which you *built* in their lives.

- What did you build with? A word? A listening ear? A gift? An affirmation? An idea?
- Can you think of ways in which you could have been a more effective answer to your own prayer to enter lives to build?

Thank the Lord for the people who have had a building ministry in your life!

Avoid Membership on the Wrecking Crew

A good thing to remember
A better thing to do
Work with the construction gang
Not with the wrecking crew![1]

Perhaps you will find this difficult to believe, but in three short days recently I was criticized three times! All unfounded remarks, of course—not one person had earned the right to criticize.

Something unsettling, even highly disturbing took place in my mind—at least I think it was in my mind. I reacted violently to those who dared to pass judgment on how I spent my time, my money and right on down to a comment on my appearance. Being a "mature Christian woman," it was definitely out of character for me to respond to criticism with a critical spirit of my own.

There were moments when I wish I never had stamped on my heart Lila Trotman's prayer, "Let me never enter a life except to build." There were no two ways about it—I was not building. I was cooperating with the demolition squad which had invaded my mind and attitude.

A critical spirit is so easily developed—and goes almost unnoticed until it gets a foothold and clouds your perspective. Women who are willing to take the risks of leadership must be on guard against this most destructive, insidious personal characteristic.

A good friend and prayer partner seemed so able to deal with this in her life, even though she was in the most vulnerable position of being the pastor's wife. In prayer times with her, how often I recall her sincere petition: "Lord, please forgive my tendency to a critical spirit. Cleanse me from any shadow of a critical attitude, that I might serve Thee blamelessly."

As I ponder this resurfacing character flaw of mine (sometimes referred to as sin), a pattern is revealed as to how such a critical spirit is formed and entrenched. Each of them begin with "I"—not exactly a surprise since it is that overwhelming protection of *self* which is at the core of most of our problems. Can you relate? Which of these have caused a critical spirit in you?

1. *Insecurity*. Whenever I begin to evaluate myself and get involved with destructive introspection, I open myself up to all manner of vain imaginations. "Why am I not better looking?" "If only I had more ability, more money or a charming ease with people!" Some of those things we have a measure of control over, but many things that make us insecure are beyond our control. We shake our fists in the face of God, complaining that He made some mistakes when He made us.

If our security is to be in Christ, who will free us from an undue preoccupation with self, then is not insecurity a rebuke to God?

Where is David's security in Psalm 16:5? _____

_____

What are three characteristics of the man who fears the Lord

in Psalm 112:7-8? _____

_____

2. *Intimidation*. The creepy, crawly, critical spirit has this second step in its development.

Nehemiah was a builder. No sooner had he arrived in Jerusalem to begin the project of rebuilding the walls around the city, when Sanballat and Tobiah became insecure and stirred up trouble. They had been given a job to do and they had not done it. Do you fall into that trap? Have you ever thought, *Either I can't or I won't do this job, but I don't want anyone more willing or qualified to do it either!*

Sanballat and Tobiah stood and watched (see Neh. 4:2) the

people who had a mind to work. The workers were organized and were carrying bricks. They saw a need and under Nehemiah's leadership, they were filling it. Tobiah and Sanballat were intimidated by the success of the effort. Are you ever intimidated by another's success? Have you heard comments like—

"She does everything so well, I won't even try!"

"I could never do as well—or look as good—or say it as cleverly."

I may as well admit it to you—there are people in my life who intimidate me! And I am not proud of it nor what it produces in my life!

A few years ago I was speaking at a conference in the East. I was in grand company as I sat next to a Christian sister who is a great woman of God, well-known speaker and magnificently used by the Lord internationally. What a privilege to become acquainted with her and other leaders at the retreat. Several hundred women sat in front of me during that first session and I felt the Lord just lift the hearts of all of us. He was doing just what He said He would do.

At a dinner held for the speakers, retreat hostesses and visiting seminar leaders, three women from a nearby state, who also had a very influential and successful ministry in retreats with women, shared their continuing need for speakers. The three women sat in the fourth row during the general sessions, and as I glanced over the crowd during my second opportunity at the podium, my eyes were drawn to them. They were whispering. Then they wrote a note or two. I knew what they were doing! They were evaluating me and what I was saying! I just knew they were deciding whether or not I was good enough. Guess what I felt? You guessed it—.

3. *Intimidation.* It crippled my communication and once I allowed my mind to be clouded and cluttered with the response of those three women to me, my ability to communicate the message God had given to the 697 others was a big zilch! Let me be quick to add that I was not the *only* one to notice it and there has not been an invitation to speak to that particular group. But my reaction disgusted me then and still does today.

I want to react like Nehemiah! Even though he was intimidated by his opponents with their snide remarks about the workers' inability to do the job and how foolish they looked trying to clear away the rubble to get to the construction site, Nehemiah sent one of his famous arrow prayers straight to heaven and kept on building. He knew that he was responsible for only his own attitude, not the attitude or actions of others. He could, however, be an influence on others' attitudes and actions in constructive ways because he was the leader. The leader's own responses, positively or negatively, *can* become contagious as the role modeling infiltrates the group.

Paul directs us to be examples of godliness in Titus 2:7-8. If we follow Scripture, what will happen to our opponents?

Well, that night I moved right along to the next step in reinforcing my critical spirit by involving myself in—

4. *Insinuation.* I blamed those women for my behavior! Yes, I subtly but firmly transferred the responsibility to them. At this point no one else has to know what is happening; it can be like a game as you think, *If they had not done this, I wouldn't have done that! If she weren't so short and cute, I wouldn't look so tall and awkward. If she were not such a great speaker, I would sound better! If my husband were as supportive as her husband, of course I would be better able to serve!* You can keep right on going, can't you, with all sorts of personal examples. *Tell me you can!* How easily we can make ourselves believe that another's actions are responsible for our response.

When we insinuate that others are responsible for our actions, what does Proverbs 21:2 offer as a checkpoint?

We have even been known to blame our foolishness on

_____ Proverbs 19:3.

5. *Insult.* There is that *I* again. Now I can begin to actually *see* that person or persons negatively. I can even get ready for the negative attitude about whatever is said, done, worn or in some cases, even *eaten* by that person. That preparation for the negative is often nothing more than self-protection.

Barbara is a person to be avoided by me. It is apparent that somehow and in some way I have intimidated her. I know you are laughing—how could anybody be intimidated by Daisy? But Barbara has the uncanny ability to come up with negative questions, tinged with patronizing overtones, negative answers and negative observations about me. "How are you doing, Daisy?"—an innocent enough question, right? But if I let her in a bit on what occupies my days, her reply will be something like, "How does your husband feel about your being away from home so much?" or "You should treat yourself to a day off to get your hair done." She is the type that, when you are as Nehemiah was—involved in a great project—she will say, "I hope you won't have to neglect your home now," or, "I know that this year's retreat is going to be so much better than last!" Immediately, flashing across my mind comes last year's project, and try as I will, I cannot imagine what was so bad about it! It is the better part of wisdom to prepare yourself for negative input, as a means of self-preservation, when those encounters occur.

Then there are those strictly personal comments: "I didn't know you sewed." (when you have just spent three weeks trying to make the latest home-sewn look store-bought!) "I tried that blouse on, but it just didn't look like it was well made, so I didn't get it. It looks nice on you, however." "Do you enjoy wearing a wig?"

My friend told me her husband calls this back-door complimenting "damnation by faint praise." This step is reinforced in *my* attitude when I insult the other person or persons by looking for their point of vulnerability and magnifying it. "She has given this same message hundreds of times—how can she get away with this lack of preparation?" "Here she is talking about children and I happen to know that hers are no angels." "She doesn't even sew—she just has all the money in the world to buy her clothes."

❀ Constructing Positive Conversation

Put a *D* in front of those you think might be destructive, and a *C* in front of those that are constructive comments.

_____1. "Do you know what we could do next year, instead?"
_____2. "Thank you for letting the Lord use you."

_____3. "I really enjoyed the banquet. Now remember that when you hear the criticism."

_____4. "You really look tired!"

_____5. "You certainly look better than the last time I saw you!"

_____6. "May I help you by praying for you?"

_____7. "Considering you had so little to work with, you have done a great job."

It really *does* take the wisdom of Solomon to know how to respond or not to respond in these volatile exchanges. Solomon has some pungent proverbs that will help:

Proverbs 12:18: _____

_____

Proverbs 18:19: _____

_____

But the last step is certainly the most destructive to the Kingdom.

6. *Influence others.* "Evil words destroy. Godly skill rebuilds" (Prov. 11:9, *TLB*). A critical spirit is destructive in my own life, but when gossip and criticism are shared with others—I enter lives to destroy and criticism is sometimes disguised as discernment. Let me give you an outrageous example.

You have just attended a symphony concert. In the party afterward, someone launches a conversation with, "Well, how did you like Beethoven tonight?" Balancing your 7-Up and petit four, you venture, "I thought it was wonderful! The music was powerfully and movingly performed, don't you think?"

Then it happens. "I thought it was good, but of course not nearly as well done as their last season in London. The cello section seemed to be out of tune, the percussion a bit weak in the last movement . . . . "

How do you feel? Like an unsophisticated know-nothing, correct? If you were up on Beethoven you would have been able to notice and discern the weaknesses. Right?

Let's try another example. You have just come from church. You say, "Wasn't that a grand service?"

"I don't think it was all that great. Didn't you notice how many mistakes the organist made?"

"Well, no, I guess I'm not that astute a musician, since I didn't notice that."

"And did you hear that prayer? If that was not self-righteous, I don't know what it was."

The critical spirit has robbed the joy from me. There is a kind of pseudo-sophistication felt even in the Church of Jesus Christ that surfaces in name-dropping and in armchair criticism of church leaders. Let's not be foolish. Discernment is not only necessary, but is a gift of God to enrich and empower our spiritual lives. Wisdom in sharing discernment, however, goes hand in hand with the use of that spiritual gift.

Do you know anyone like the one pictured in Proverbs 12:18? Take a walk through several chapters in Proverbs and note a dozen verses that have to do with your conversation and your influence on others.

Women of God, let our prayer be for forgiveness for any critical spirit that begins with a feeling of *insecurity*. This vulnerability leads to being *intimidated* because others "do so well." "If she wasn't so capable, I wouldn't show up so poorly," says the one who *insinuates* that the other person is somehow responsible for her own behavior. *Insults* build up inside as thoughts are allowed to invade the mind like, "Nobody could have it that much together—you can see she needs to lose 10 pounds, there is evidently no discipline in her life." Then the cement of the *influence* of others is added. You are committed to behave according to the words of your mouth in criticism. You find it difficult to change and your attitude demands that you ask forgiveness of God, appropriating His power to change your attitude.

The thing that troubles me so much as I face the criticism of others, is that I sense the critical spirit being formed in me. Leaders are particularly open to this problem because they take risks that tend to draw criticism. God has forgiven and is continuing to cleanse, and I thank and praise Him for this provision for my sin.

Ralph Carmichael told my husband that he has discovered a

confirmation that God is doing a work in his life. He is a musician, publisher, composer, arranger and director. He is therefore, also a critic. Hundreds of pieces of music cross his desk annually, many sent by aspiring composers. He said, "It was a moment of deep joy when I realized that I was as happy about another musician's success as my own!"

Scriptural Blueprints

Look up the following Scripture references and match the reference to the destructive steps in the formation of a critical spirit:

James 4:11-12	Insecurity
Nehemiah 4:2	
Proverbs 9:11	Intimidation
Ruth 1:11-13	
Matthew 7:5	Insinuation
Proverbs 6:19	Insult
Proverbs 11:11	Influence others
Proverbs 11:13	

Some Proverbs that can be building blocks:

Proverbs 23:12 _____

_____

Proverbs 25:12 _____

_____

Proverbs 12:24 _____

_____

Block Your Loose Talk

Remind your people of these great facts, and command them in the name of the Lord not to argue over unimportant things. Such arguments are confusing and useless, and even harmful. Steer clear of foolish discussions which lead people into the sin of anger with each other (2 Tim. 2:14,16, *TLB*).

Malettor Cross is a grand, black workman and mother of 11 children. She and her husband Haman serve the Lord through their Detroit Afro-American Mission. It was a choice opportunity for me to meet her and then to get to know her as we shared a speaking assignment in Northern Michigan.

"In our one-room church in Tennessee, four classes met in four corners, but the 'old folks' always got the choir loft. In that clapboard sanctuary I received the only Sunday School training I can remember.

"'Okay, Brother, hear it again! God who at sundry times and in divers manners, spake in time past . . . '"

"'Just a minute, Brother, you have talked too much. Let's hear from the preacher now!

"'Well, friends, let us consider this passage from another angle.

"'"God, who at sundry times and in divers manners spake in time past unto the fathers by the prophets, hath in these last days spoken unto us by *his* Son'" (Heb. 1:1-2, *KJV*).

"This was about as divers a manner as God had ever spoken in, and I sat on the edge of my seat to listen to the outcome of the argument. Really it wasn't an argument, but a four-cornered pooling of ignorance. The winner was the loudest shouter.

"The only verse I can remember learning as a child is Hebrews 1:1-2. God has been dealing with me in 'divers' manners ever since I accepted Jesus as my Saviour when I was 11 years old."[2]

Malettor continued to share with me her fascinating pilgrimage plus her desire to rightly divide the Word without vain arguments. God is using her to do just that!

The Word is your tool. Use it not in useless haggling, but work hard to be worthy of the "well done." Essentially these verses tell us not to talk so much and for some of us that is hard work.

The good workman is true to the Scriptures. He does not falsify it. Nor does he try to confuse people, like Elymas the sorcerer, by "making crooked the straight paths of the Lord" (see Acts 13:10).

"On the contrary, he handles the Word with such scrupulous care that he both stays on the path himself, keeping to the highway and avoiding the byways, and makes it easy for others to follow.["3]

BE A CONSTRUCTIVE WORKMAN

Now, back to the Word for a look at those steps to being a *constructive* influence. We are to be workmen that have no need to be ashamed of critical and destructive attitudes and actions. There are several lists in Scripture of the qualities of one who builds up, and 2 Peter 1:5-8 and 10 (*TLB*, italics added), presents a ladder toward the character of Christ within us.

> But to obtain these gifts, you need more than faith; you must also work hard to be good, and even that is not enough. For then you must learn to know God better and discover what he wants you to do. Next, learn to put aside your own desires so that you will become patient and godly, gladly letting God have his way with you. This will make possible the next step, which is for you to enjoy other people and to like them, and finally you will grow to love them deeply.
> The more you go on in this way, the more you will grow strong spiritually and become fruitful and useful to our Lord Jesus Christ. . . . So, dear brothers, work hard to prove that you really are among those God has called and chosen.

The Workman's Ladder

The bottom step is *faith*. If your faith has brought you through to a knowledge of Jesus Christ as your Saviour, and if you can claim His promises, then add to your faith step two:

Goodness. Fix your thoughts and mind on being good. Ethel Barrett has written a book entitled *Don't Look Now—But Your Personality Is Showing,* and in it she relates a struggle she had with the old-fashioned attribute of goodness.

A young woman came to me without a job and without a Saviour and very, very broke, materially and spiritually. I introduced her to Christ, gave her some clothes and a wee bit of money, and by some miracle I had a contact that landed her a job as a clerk in a department store. I blessed her and prayed with her and sent her on her way. And I felt so noble I could hardly stand it.

Two years later she phoned me. She'd made out well, and was now a buyer of women's clothing in another city. She was just passing through. Did I want to have lunch? I did. I could hardly wait to hear her out-pourings of gratitude and to give her some more encouragement, peppered with my wisdom and counsel.

The jolt came when I met her in a downtown restaurant. She had more money on her back in one outfit than I could afford to spend in a year . . . She pulled off her kid gloves. I pulled off my cotton gloves. She looked at me, wide-eyed, and said,

"Hasn't the Lord been wonderful?"

Full-blown, into my mind it came. All at once, and more quickly than it can be told. "What do you mean, the Lord? *Me* and the Lord. I gave you money . . . . "

I gave *that* to the Lord at once in the same flash with which it had come to me, and I am more ashamed of it than of many more heinous crimes I've committed. Telling about it takes a paragraph; actually it was only a twinge. But the implications of that twinge are horrendous![4]

Let us swiftly release anything that is not good as we add goodness to our faith.

Step three is *knowledge*. Hosea 6:3 *(TLB)* says: "Oh, that we might know the Lord! Let us press on to know him, and he will respond to us as surely as the coming of dawn or the rain of early spring." The workman pursues knowledge and is discontent in the present level of intimacy with the Lord, but presses on to know Him. The hymn writer has penned a prayer to be sung:

More about Jesus would I know,
More of His grace to others show;
More of His saving fullness see,
More of His love who died for me.

More about Jesus let me learn,
More of His holy will discern;
Spirit of God, my teacher be,
Showing the things of Christ to me.

More about Jesus; in His word,
Holding communion with my Lord;
Hearing His voice in every line,
Making each faithful saying mine.[5]

The next rung on the ladder is *self-control*. Isn't it good to know that we can cooperate with God in building this quality into our life and leadership? It is a characteristic of the fruit of His life within us, according to Galatians 5:22, and this is not something we can drum up or work for. It is the product of the work of the Holy Spirit as we submit to Him. Hurray! But, we can cooperate with the process. A wiser man than any of us expressed it this way in Proverbs 16:32 *(TLB)*: "It is better to have self-control than to control an army." (I do better in self-control against an army than confronted with a hot fudge sundae!) From self-control we move on to—

Perseverance—which is step five. It is also called stick-to-itiveness. Be the builder who is not too quick to turn over the job to someone else. Patiently learn to build right there on your part of the wall and you will move on up the ladder to *godliness*.

Godliness (step six) will include the development of holy habits—consistent church involvement, quiet times with the Lord, speaking the truth in love to everyone and others. Can you name more?

Step seven is *kindness*. In *The Living Bible* it is said that one who is kind "enjoys other people." My mother-in-love exuded kindness. A woman of great spiritual strength and influence, she plainly enjoyed people. Perhaps the most important reason I trusted her so much was the fact that she spoke kindly of everyone. After my husband and I had been married just a couple of years, she presented me with a beautiful afghan she had thoughtfully crocheted during the many long hours of her and Dad's traveling ministry. Her kindness was backed up with the knowledge that I was not being "run down," or destroyed by any word of hers "behind the wall." Because I had never heard her criticize another, there was no reason to think that she would speak unkindly of me. That knowledge was a far more precious gift to me than the afghan, though few others would likely know of the unspoken gift. Kindness in any form is a character quality to be pursued, don't you think?

Love is step eight in the constructive ladder of Christlike qualities for the workman. It is a 1 Corinthians love. This chapter became real to me when someone pointed out that this is simply the way in which Christ loves us. Build love into other's lives in the same proportion Christ has loved you!

Never let it be said that we have discouraged others from leadership because of the criticism of those who are now leading. Who would want to be in that spot—to receive or attract criticism? As we serve and lead, let's enjoy the exertion of moving higher, rising not on the materialistic ladder of success by the world's standards but on the ladder toward God that will make us increasingly effective.

All have a share in the beauty, all have a part in the plan.
What does it matter what duty falls to the lot of a man?
Someone has blended the plaster;
    someone has carried the stone;
Neither the man nor the Master ever has builded alone;
Make a roof for the weather,
    building a house for the King;
Only by working together have men
    accomplished a thing.[6]

Work Up the Ladder

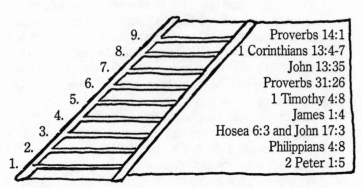

9. Proverbs 14:1
8. 1 Corinthians 13:4-7
7. John 13:35
6. Proverbs 31:26
5. 1 Timothy 4:8
4. James 1:4
3. Hosea 6:3 and John 17:3
2. Philippians 4:8
1. 2 Peter 1:5

Look up the verse noted and find the character quality mentioned that leads up the rungs to the top. Be sure you know the wall your ladder of success is leaning against!

❀ How Should I Respond to Criticism?

The Apostle Paul was criticized for many things, some of which follow:

1. He was accused of being indecisive (see 2 Cor. 1:17-18).
2. He was accused of being untrustworthy and mishandling funds (see 2 Cor. 8:20).
3. He was accused of being worldly (see 2 Cor. 10:1; 2:5).
4. He was accused of being an unimpressive man (see 2 Cor. 10:10).
5. He was accused of being an unskilled orator (see 2 Cor. 11:6).
6. He was accused of being unqualified to teach (see 2 Cor. 11:5).
7. He was accused of having a lack of dignity (see 2 Cor. 11:7-9).
8. He was accused of being deceitful and taking advantage of people (see 2 Cor. 7:2-4).

What was Paul's response to these accusations? He loved his accusors! Read 2 Corinthians 1:6,14,23; 2:4; 6:11; 12:15.[7]

✿ Life's Task

Isn't it strange that princes and kings,
    And clowns that caper in sawdust rings
And common folks like you and me
    Are builders for eternity?

To each is given a bag of tools,
    A shapeless mass and a book of rules,
And each must make, ere life was flown,
    A stumbling block—or a stepping stone.[8]

Contracting with the Lord

✿ The Terms of the Building Contract

"Let me show you what the man who comes to me, hears what I have to say, and puts it into practice, is really like. He is like a man building a house, who dug down to rock-bottom and laid the foundation of his house upon it. Then when the flood came and the flood-water swept down upon that house, it could not shift it because it was properly built" (Luke 6:48, *Phillips*).

✿ The Price

"Suppose one of you wants to build a tower. Will he not first sit down and estimate the cost to see if he has enough money to complete it?" (Luke 14:28, *NIV*).

Consider what it might cost you to be a subcontractor who is willing to work hard when building. You who have assumed any leadership roles at all will be shaking your heads violently when the *prices* of being a workman are discussed. There are costs to be contended with in serving the Lord—out front. One of those prices is in your vulnerability to criticism. Perhaps you have begun to pay. Consider carefully the price!

The Guarantee

"Then every workman who has built on the foundation with the right materials, and whose work still stands, will get his pay" (1 Cor. 3:14, *TLB*).

The Contractor

"Unless the Lord builds a house, the builders' work is useless" (Ps. 127:1, *TLB*).

O Lord,
You know how much I long to work for you—
For you have done so much within the heart of me.
I must begin somewhere though talents may seem few
Because there are about me needs I see.
Perhaps I've been a bit too timid, Lord,
Afraid to reach, to touch another life through mine.
What joy that reaching, touching can afford
When I join hands with Thee in work divine.[9]

BE A W.O.W.!

> "Study *and* be eager *and* do your utmost to present yourself to God approved (tested by trial), a workman who has no cause to be ashamed, correctly analyzing *and* accurately dividing—rightly handling and skillfully teaching—the Word of Truth" (2 Tim. 2:15, *AMP*).

This is a tall order, but if you have your tools ready God will find you work. But what is God's work?

The work is the proper application of the Word of God. That is how I would like most to be introduced: as a W.O.W.! A woman of the Word.

Some of you in my age group—physically or spiritually—have to admit that we have spent years and years in the Word. Some of us have attended and/or taught dozens, even hundreds, of Bible studies over the years. Some of us have even dared to regard our study of the Word as a spiritual safety zone. It is comfortable to believe that when we are studying and reading, we are more spiritual than when we are washing dishes, playing tennis or serving on a phone committee for a coming election.

That had better not be so! We are either God's women, regardless of the activity, or we are not God's women at all. What I do does *not* make me more or less spiritual. When I received Jesus as my Saviour and my resident, live-in Lord, and when the Holy Spirit came to dwell in me, my life was opened up spiritually. I became a spiritual woman.

❀ Builder's Code

In the middle verses of Psalm 19, there are six sections of three parts each that confirm the revelation of God through His Word. The Scripture is titled six different ways, followed by an attribute of the Word, and then how the Word of God should affect our lives. Work it out for yourself.

	Title	Attribute	Effect
v. 7	_____	_____	_____
	_____	_____	_____
v. 8	_____	_____	_____
	_____	_____	_____
v. 9	_____	_____	_____
	_____	_____	_____

If you would like to be an approved workman you will want to have a systematic personal Bible study commitment. A resource guide for this time which is widely used is the *Daily Walk*, published by *Walk Thru the Bible Ministries*, Inc., P.O. Box 720653, Atlanta, GA 30358. It is a plan for reading the entire Bible through in a year. It is without a doubt the most helpful, complete and usable plan I have found. Several organizations and denominations also offer the *Daily Walk* through their own ministries.

Bible study is not an end in itself, however. It is a facilitator to holy living. God has planned that His precious Word be applied after thorough study and prayerful consideration. The Word is to be obeyed, not just observed.

As we implement the Word into our lives and our ministries, great care must be taken to make the applications in context. A sense of humor is a must as we hear of situations complicated by WRONGLY dividing the Word of truth.

A certain seven-year-old approached his father and said, "Daddy, when we sin we get smaller, don't we?"

"No," replied the dad. "Why do you say that?"

"Well," he exclaimed, "the Bible says, 'All have sinned and come short!'"

Or, a Sunday School teacher reported that the excuse the little girl gave for not having her memory work complete was "because the only copy of the Bible we have at home is the reversed version."

Paul, in writing his letter to Timothy, reminds him that the whole Bible was given to us from God and is designed by the Holy Spirit to accomplish several specific things in our lives.

Look it up and fill in the blanks—come on—I know it is work, but do it! It is good for you!

"The whole Bible . . . is useful to _____ us

what is true and to _____ what is wrong n

our lives; it _____ and _____ us

do what is right. It is God's way of making us

_____ at every point, _____ to

do good to everyone" (2 Tim. 3:16-17, *TLB*).

The Biblical Workman

1. Find some reasons why we study the Bible. Psalm 119 will suggest many things the Scripture will do for you. List at least a dozen of them:

2. Necessary ingredients to leading a Bible study, writing a Bible study, or as a matter of fact, attending a Bible study:

Preparation—Homework, study, work hard (2 Tim. 2:15)
Involvement—Open-heartedness both to the Word and to
     one another (Col. 3:16)
Enthusiasm—the *en theos* brand of enthusiasm (Col. 3:23)

3. Tools might include: The Bible—various versions and trans-
                              lations
                            Commentaries
                            Christian books and biographies
4. Now, let's build a Bible study:

"God, in his kindness, has taught me how to be an expert builder. I have laid the foundation and Apollos has built on it. But he who builds on the foundation must be very careful. And no one can ever lay any other real foundation than that one we already have—Jesus Christ. But there are various kinds of materials that can be used to build on that founda-tion. Some use gold and silver and jewels; and some build with sticks, and hay, or even straw! There is going to come a time of testing at Christ's Judgment Day to see what kind of material each builder has used. Everyone's work will be put through the fire so that all can see whether or not it keeps its value, and what was really accomplished (1 Cor. 3:10-13, *TLB*).

What nursery story do these verses remind you of? Right! The three little pigs! Remember how they set out to build their houses and each bought the stuff to build? First, the straw, then the wood, and finally the smart little pig built his house of bricks. When the big bad wolf came to huff and to puff and to try to blow down the brick house, he was stymied and had to climb up on the roof to come down through the chimney. He plopped right into the kettle of boiling water the wise little pig had waiting for him!

First Corinthians 3 tells us to be careful what we use to build with—not wood, hay and stubble, but the precious stones that will last throughout eternity.

I have already given you some of my ideas on *The Three Little Pigs,* but you take it from here. Create a Bible study by doing the following:

1. Read *The Three Little Pigs* again.
2. Find three biblical principles in the story.
3. Using a concordance, locate some Scripture passages to illustrate the principles.
4. Just for fun—try to illustrate your outline!

Try this with nursery rhymes—brainstorming with a group.
For example: Little Boy Blue, come blow your horn.
There was an old woman,
who lived in a shoe.
Mary, Mary quite contrary,
how does your garden grow?

Back to the little pigs. The day will come when our work will be tried. Let us be sure not to be duped into thinking we can be a modern Miss Piggy who builds with stuff that just doesn't stand up to the onslaughts of the big bad wolf.

Be a workman who builds for the long haul, without short-cuts, who places bricks of Christian character, commitment to prayer and planning and love for the lost and poor. Wood, hay and stubble building is akin to the let's-have-a-dilly-of-a-program-this-year leadership pattern that lacks purpose, goals and ministry.

God is both Architect and Carpenter and He will use any of us hammers and saws to build.

The Construction Crew Bible Study Sample

Nehemiah is a builder. Read the 13 chapters of his story and then organize a Bible study. Here are some helps to help begin the project:

1. Date: 444 B.C.

2. Nehemiah opens and closes with prayer. Work is his companion! See Nehemiah 6:3.

3. Chapters 1-6—Reconstruction
   Chapters 7-13—reinstruction

4. What do you learn about Nehemiah in Chapter 1?

   His position _____ His quest _____

   His commitment _____ His qualifications _____

5. Four months pass between Nehemiah 1:1 and 2:1 while he waits on God.
   Then, Nehemiah was Sent—2:5
                     Safe—2:9
                     Supplied—2:8

6. The people had a mind to work. "Let us arise and build!" they cried. They began by building near their own homes. (See Neh. 3:28.)

7. Can you discover the significance of the 10 gates in the wall of Jerusalem?

8. Can you identify with the problem confronted in Nehemiah 4:10? Do you have any idea what you can do about it?

9. Some say that Nehemiah 4:14 is the key verse of the story. What do you think? If you had been among the workers, what assignment would you have wished for as Nehemiah organized the project—in the face of the opposition?

10. What character quality was evidenced in Nehemiah's response in 5:6? Is this respect for *your* work for God clearly evident in your life and service?

11. What a day's schedule is outlined in chapter 8! What part of the day or weeks' activities would have been a highlight for you?

12. Chapter 9 describes another Festival and a prayer of repentance. Nehemiah 9:38 is a phrase to remember—a declaration of intent based on past experience and knowledge and a commitment to service. Can you make it your own?

Can you see how these ideas were lifted from these chapters? Just for yourself or for sharing as the Lord gives opportunity, try with another book of Scripture. Use imagery and creativity in your presentation—sketches or artwork add the right touch.

Some Guidelines for Bible Classes

1. HOW TO START
   a. Know the Bible has the answer (see 2 Tim. 3:16-17).
   b. Burden for the need of women in your area or church (see Rom. 16:26).
   c. Gather a friend or friends who share this concern and with whom you can pray about starting a study or Bible class.
   d. Pray for God's choice of women to attend the class.

e. Be willing to start with just a few.

f. Do not put off the starting date—strike while the iron is hot.

g. Pray for God's choice for a teacher for your class—realizing it might be YOU!

h. If no trained teacher is available, pray for a choice of materials which could be used and the leadership shared.

2. HOW LONG TO HOLD THE CLASS

a. Decide on beginning and ending dates. These will often be based on the length of the study undertaken.

b. Reevaluate the situation—continue as you are led.

c. A committee should make this decision even if it consists of only the teacher and the hostess.

3. WHERE AND WHEN TO HOLD THE STUDY

a. Consider using the facilities of your church, emphasizing the nursery possibilities. No one has to clean her home and make it a special place to be!

b. Neighborhood groups are often held in homes, but be careful to arrange for nursery services.

c. Decide on a starting hour and a finishing one and stick to it!

4. HOW TO CONDUCT THE CLASS

a. Have *one* regular teacher, if possible.

b. Have a hostess who is on her toes to greet, welcome newcomers and have name tags. Can you think of some more qualifications for a hostess?

5. SUGGESTED ORDER OF CLASS

a. Have leader call for prayer by someone she knows will not be embarrassed or pray herself.

b. Announcements—welcome—introductions—an ice-breaker.

c. Lesson

d. Brief question period if teacher is qualified. Set a firm time limit for this.

e. Bible study assignment for next time. Do not embarrass but *motivate!*

6. POINTERS TO PONDER
   a. Keep classes fresh and informal but not *too* informal.
   b. Don't scold or embarrass absentees; they have not
      pledged regularity.

AIM FOR THE "WELL DONE"

Amy Carmichael was a teenager in Northern Ireland just a few years before she set out for the Orient to eventually become the founder of Dohnavur Fellowship in Southern India.

It was a windy, damp day as Amy and her family were on their way home from church. Shocked to see an old woman in rags, struggling alone with a heavy bundle, young Amy thought surely the woman should have been in church!

Suddenly Amy turned and ran after the older woman, took her by the arm and carried the burden for her. The onlookers laughed to see this incongruous team and Amy burned red with embarrassment. Misery threatened to engulf her—wet, sad, hurt and humiliated—but the Spirit of God recalled 1 Corinthians 3:13 *(NIV)* to her mind: "The fire will test the quality of each man's work."

A phrase came to her heart that was to become one of her life mottoes: NOTHING IS IMPORTANT SAVE THAT WHICH IS ETERNAL.

Amy Carmichael, in her life's work of rescuing and serving India's temple children as well as in writing deep devotional books for building in the lives of millions, is a model of a workman who did not need to be ashamed! The praise or taunts of men are not worthy building materials. The favor of her heavenly Father and the knowledge of the approval of her Lord— these would be her motives and motivations. She would lay up treasure in heaven.

Amy Carmichael would have been the last one to classify herself as a leader by the standards of this world. But a servant-leader, according to the principles of the Word of God, she surely was! She writes of Calvary love in her classic volume *If.* It is not a book to be glanced at or read in one sitting, though it contains only several hundred words. It is a collection of thought and prayer starters. Let me share one that fits right here:

If one whose help I greatly need appears to be as content to build in wood, hay, stubble, as in gold, silver, precious stones, and I hesitate to obey my light and do without that help because so few will understand, then I know nothing of Calvary love."[10]

There is often a loneliness in leadership and Amy Carmichael knew that loneliness but was never alone. Her work had been planned for her before the beginning of time and nothing less than a lifelong commitment to building for eternity, regardless of the support or lack of it from those around her, was satisfactory.

"Work hard so God can say to you, 'Well done.'"

🎴 Creative Brickworking

What can you do with a brick besides throw it?

It was Sunday School time. We had spent weeks peering at the building project and Nehemiah's work crew through the sidewalk peepholes. "How shall we get involved?" I asked the class.

I know! A great thought came to me in a hurry.

A wheelbarrow load of rough, new, red clay bricks was brought into the circle. I explained, "Everyone take home a brick and think about how you can make it useful. Then do it—and bring it back to show us what you have done."

Next Sunday arrived and the entire group of unashamed workmen entered the basement room. Enthusiasm ran high! Imagine mature Christian adults, some a bit ho-hum about Sunday School, who could hardly wait for their show and tell opportunity! First, Leo opened his box and produced a cleverly painted paperweight. Then there were crewel-covered bricks for doorstops and bookends. One even became an unnamed Pet Brick!

Barbara produced a Brick Mother. Here's how:

1. Start with a clay brick, the older and more porous, the better.
2. Mound potting mix 2½ to 3 inches on top of the brick.
3. Set brick in a flat pan of water.
4. Flatten the top a bit and tap seeds into the one or two grooves you have made.

5. Pat soil mix to cover the seeds and remember to refill the pan with water as needed. Do not water your seedlings from overhead. The brick will absorb the water and the plants will sprout. Transplant after a few weeks.

6. Stand in amazement at the versatility of a brick!

Perhaps the prize, however, went to Katherine. She had carefully glued neatly trimmed scraps of carpeting on to her brick. Timidly she stepped up front to read the words she had typed on a card to interpret her carpet-covered brick—

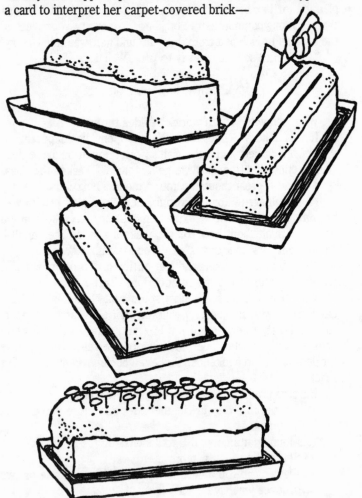

Just a Brick, But—

Underneath the overhang
    of the LOWER cupboard
Is the just-right-space
Where I rest
Until *I* can be of service.

For just above the lower cupboard
    is another
    called the UPPER
With shelves
    Up
    Up two inches
        above the reach of kitchen help
Who need the pitchers
Which rest there
Until *they* can be of service.

Thus, in my padded, prostrate state
    I serve
    as just a lowly step
To bring the family members
Within reach of HIGHER levels.
P.S. Many of my kind serve only
    to HOLD UP the SHELVES
        on LOWER levels
    for books and boots and shoes.[11]

Gold Bricks for Goodness' Sake

Here is an idea which doesn't cost much and it will be a continual reminder to you of something really special. My friend, Barbara Johnson (you remember, the special lady who has written *Where Does a Mother Go to Resign?* and is about to have a new book released entitled, *Fresh Elastic for Stretched Out Moms*—don't you love it?!) gave me this idea and says you must first do this for yourself and then—only then—reach out to others.

First get yourself a brick.

Find one around the house or buy one at a builders' supply place. Also purchase some bright, shiny *gold* wrapping paper and wrap this brick carefully in the gold paper.

Tie a colorful bow on it with some cherries or berries or other colors of spring. Now you have a beautiful *gold brick* to use as a doorstop, but mainly to remind you that *you are gold in the making!*

The furnace of pain you have come through, or are going through, has made you as *gold* for the Master's use! You have been and are being refined, purified, tried—made *worthy!* Do you know that if all the gold in the *whole* world were melted down into a solid cube, it would be about the size of an eight-room house? If you got possession of all of it, you could not buy a friend, character, peace of mind, a clear conscience or eternal life!

Now, after you have your nice shiny gold brick nicely sitting by your door as a stopper, get another one!

Wrap this brick with the same gold paper and sprig of flowers. Now select a good friend, who perhaps has been a gold brick in your life, one who has refreshed and encouraged you and may need some lifting in her life right now.

Take that shiny gold brick to her.

Tell her how she has blessed you during your testing time.

Before long, you will be making your gold bricks by the dozen and spreading this idea to others.

All the time you will be refreshing *them,* but making yourself aware of so many friends who are like gold in your own life!

Look, You're a Vessel!

A VESSEL'S PURPOSE AND PROCESS

In a wealthy home there are dishes made of gold and silver as well as some made from wood and clay. The expensive dishes are used for guests, and the cheap ones are used in the kitchen or to put garbage in. If you stay away from sin you will be like one of these dishes made of purest gold—the very best in the house—so that Christ himself can use you for his highest purposes (2 Tim. 2:20-21, *TLB*).

"Next week, everyone bring a vessel and you'll be surprised what we'll do with it!" The 40 children in front of me had a gleam in their eyes as they contemplated our next meeting's possibilities.

Then Bobby piped up, "What is a vessel anyway, Daisy?"

"Anything that can hold something, I guess, Bobby. So bring something you think might be a vessel and we'll see if it works. Use your imagination. Look all around the grounds or ask your cottage mother."

David and I were at the children's home. Of the 130 children on the grounds of the 700-acre site in the rolling hills of northern California, I had the happy opportunity to lead almost half of them in the Sunday evening service. I was trying to teach the boys and girls about how God can use each of us and what a privilege it is to be a vessel for Him.

Next Sunday arrived and so did the kids and the vessels—rusty tin cans, empty pop bottles, chipped cups, flower pots—

every size and shape imaginable. We lined them all up on the mantel of the fireplace. My idea was to put a sweet potato into each of them, fill them with water and let the kids observe and enjoy the quickly growing vines.

The water flowed and the kids decided they wanted to do it all themselves. The pitchers were filled in the rest rooms and water poured into the vessels. Whoops! We discovered vessels that were not usable. The water flowed down over the bricks, into the fireplace and all over the floor.

We managed to salvage a couple dozen that were watertight and I deposited a many-eyed sweet potato into each one. The kids watched to see if the potatoes would sprout on the spot. We waited until the next week—and the next. I could not decide why the leaves had not emerged from the vessels.

We found out! We arrived for our Sunday evening class two weeks later and the smell in the room was overpowering! The potatoes were blobs of rotten stuff and we were crushed. The lesson was a bit less than effective as far as the children were concerned, but *I* learned a great deal.

The condition of the vessel is of utmost importance: the vessel must be clean. All the rust and residue in the variety of vessels the children had offered worked to rot the contents. The container had a greater influence on the contents than we realized.

If you were to glance in your concordance, you would see how often references are made to clay, the potter, vessels and to usefulness. Five kinds of vessels are described from which I will illustrate characteristics and uses that God might have in mind for you.

Earthen Vessels

Tucked into the many, many word pictures of Paul's letters to the Corinthians is this verse: "This priceless treasure we hold, so to speak, in common earthenware—to show that the splendid power of it belongs to God and not to us" (2 Cor. 4:7, *Phillips*).

When we submit to the wooing power of the Lord and receive Jesus by faith, we become earthen vessels. We begin to understand our new life and that we have been created for a purpose—to be a container for the Spirit of God. We have been formed to contain a priceless treasure—the power of God and the message of the love of Jesus. And He will use us, even though we have been newly formed.

Have you ever seen a potter at work? He picks up the lump of clay and begins to shape it to his liking. He presses and pokes and pulls and spins it on his wheel. The product reflects the skill of the potter.

My friend Carol received the "desire of her heart" for her birthday. The potter's wheel was carefully installed in the basement right next to the washer and dryer. It was tagged, "With love from your family." She didn't have to look for excuses to wash and dry everything in sight! She used every opportunity to sit up high on the attached metal stool, place a blob of wet clay on the round table top of the potter's wheel and gather momentum by pressing the pedal beneath. It took a lot more coordination than she had at first! But, practicing over and over again, she was finally able to have "thrown a pot" (that's what they call it!) that she was willing to let her family take a look at.

It was several weeks before most of us even knew Carol had the contraption in her cellar! Then, some of her handiwork began to be received as gifts by women in the church.

At first, she wasn't sure what the finished product would be good for, but as her skill improved, she was able to plan ahead. Do you see that the Master Potter has no trial and error vessels marked with His name? He does *not* need to throw us back because He has not changed His mind!

An important lesson to be learned when submitting to the work of God in our lives is that of acceptance—in the size and shape of this vessel called us.

"When a craftsman makes anything he doesn't expect it to turn around and say, 'Why did you make me like this?' The potter, for instance, has complete control over the clay, making with one part of the lump a lovely vase, and with another a pipe for sewage (Rom. 9:21, *Phillips*).

God already knows the reasons why we have been made just the way we have and the use He will put us to. We have been designed with His will in mind!

After the clay is dry, the potter fires the vessel. Did you know vessels made by potters in Bible times that were fired once were used for storing grain or other dry foods? A water jug—or vessel of honor—must be fired again before it can be used. It must also be glazed. A clay pot is good for growing plants, but its use is limited because it is porous. It takes on much of the character of its contents.

Remember that the vessel is the only figure in 2 Timothy 2 that is inanimate. It is not as easy to identify with this one—but there are no flesh and blood foibles to consider, either! The imagery needs life for most of us to realize that the vessel must *choose* to be used. We *do* have the freedom to withhold ourselves from the Potter's shelf, from the work of the kitchen or even from being a channel or a sewer pipe!

Do the words of this old poem encourage you to make yourself available to Jesus?

> The Master stood in His garden
> among the lilies fair,
> Which His own hand had planted and trained
> with tend'rest care.
> He looked at their snowy blossoms and marked
> with observant eye
> That His flowers were sadly drooping for their leaves
> were parched and dry.
> "My lilies need to be watered," the Heavenly
> Master said;
> "Wherein shall I draw it for them, and raise each
> drooping head?"
> Close to His feet on the pathway, empty and
> frail and small,
> An earthen vessel was lying, which seemed
> of no use at all.
> But the Master saw, and raised it from the
> dust in which it lay,
> And smiled as He gently whispered: "This shall
> do my work today."
> "It is but an earthen vessel, but it lay so
> close to me;

It is small, but it is empty, and that is all it needs to be."
So to the fountain He took it, and filled it to the brim;
How glad was the earthen vessel to be of
    some use to Him!
He poured forth the living water over His lilies fair,
Until the vessel was empty, and again He filled it there.
He watered the drooping lilies until they revived again,
And the Master saw with pleasure, that His labor
    was not in vain.
His own hand had drawn the water which refreshed
    the thirsty flowers
But He used the earthen vessel to convey
    the living showers.
And to itself it whispered, as He laid it aside once more.
"Still will I lie in His pathway, Just where I did before.
Close would I be to the Master and empty would
    I remain.
Some day He may use me to water His flowers again."[1]

But there is more for the woman who is willing to be further shaped and fired for additional service.

Vessels of Honor and Dishonor

I have been told that the waterjug occupied a very obvious position in front of every rural Palestinian home. Near the front doorstep was the vessel of honor and at the opposite side the vessel of dishonor was located. Fresh water was daily brought from the well in the village and the vessel of honor was filled. All waste was placed in the vessel of dishonor.

Second Timothy 2:20 describes these vessels. The vessel of honor had to be kept scrupulously clean. It was used only for fresh water and served as a sign of hospitality. Besides the family, travelers were refreshed from this jug. The water was also used for cleansing.

How do the vessels of honor and dishonor differ from the earthen vessel? They have been to the fire a second time. There is also a glaze that not only keeps the clay from absorbing the water but also acts as a thermal agent. Paul says of the vessel of honor, "If a man keeps himself clean from the contaminations of evil he will be a vessel used for honourable purposes, dedicated and serviceable for the use of the master of the household" (2 Tim. 2:21, *Phillips*).

The vessel of dishonor has also been fired twice but it is used for refuse. It often looks the same on the outside but all that is poured into it is dirty or left over. Cleanliness is unimportant to this vessel.

"Whatever He says to you, do it!" The mother of Jesus at the festive wedding in Cana gave that direction to the servants. It must have been an orthodox home as well as a rather wealthy one, for there were six waterpots standing there, each holding 20 to 30 gallons. Those were vessels! Jesus used these vessels of honor to reveal His power and to begin His public ministry.

Imagine being submissive enough to be willing to fill the waterpots to the tune of 140 gallons!

"Do you mean Lord, that we need 140 gallons of water?"

"Whatever He says to you, do it!"

But Jesus had done no miracles yet. No storm had been stilled, no little girl raised from the dead, no crowd had been fed; there was no track record of success. A real act of faith was needed to fill those pots!

Could the Lord have produced the wine without the effort of filling those jugs? Could He have done the miracle without their help?

Of course, He could. But—

Instead, He gave those servants and the wedding guests the opportunity to have a part in the miracle—to fill the waterpots, to stand by and see God revealing Himself through this celebration. He does the same for each of us—even when the situation is all out of control. Listen to Him. He can perform miracles without your help, but don't miss the opportunity to follow His instructions when He chooses to allow you to cooperate with Him.

"This first of His signs (miracles, wonderworks) Jesus performed in Cana of Galilee and manifested His glory—by it He displayed His greatness *and* His power openly; and His disciples believed in Him—adhered to, trusted in and relied on Him" (John 2:11, *AMP*).

They believed that He was the One they had waited for.

I want to be a vessel of honor, but I also want to be the obedient servant.

Again we see that the image is flexible. It is apparent that we can be responsible for the contents of this vessel—although it is an inanimate object—in order that the lesson the Scripture teaches can be applied.

For example, we can *choose* to take another step in usability.

Chosen Vessels

These vessels have gone through the fire several times. There are often special markings and designs on the finish of these jars or vases. If the potter wants to make a gift to you, he may say, "Here is my choice for you. Take this one: it will never put me to shame. Take this vessel to your home—it reflects the skill of the maker. It is a chosen vessel."

Do you know a chosen vessel? Chosen vessels are those who have been made stronger because of the fire. They gleam and shine with the design of God in their lives. It is as if they have been stamped with the mark of the Maker.

Many of my prayer partners are chosen vessels.

Lucille Erickson is one of my special friends. Just a few years my senior, she is less than five feet tall and weighs about half of what I do. A couple of years ago one of her eyes had to be removed. Did that stop her? Not for a minute—well, maybe for a minute or two. But she has been through the fire more often than most of us. Because of the many firings, she is stronger and more useful. Her wit and determination are beyond my comprehension. Dragging herself out of bed, she arranges parties for "old folks," most of whom are more able than she is. Cutting up old greeting cards and cleverly reassembling them doesn't sound like a very high level activity for Jesus' sake. But when Lucille sends one to me with a love note inside, this old vessel of mine quivers with the knowledge that I have been remembered and prayed for. When the Indian church in Minneapolis burned to the ground last year, who spearheaded a relief operation? You're right, Lucille! And if it is possible to have a ministry through needlework and note writing, then Lucille has found it. She is clean, filled and available for miracles to be worked in her. She's a chosen vessel, indeed.

Lucille and I share a penchant for Ziggy, the loser. Lucy clipped a particularly appropriate cartoon and sent it to me. Ziggy is pictured flat on his back, puffing and panting and saying, "My energy level reached its peak two years ago—but I think I slept through it!" She must depend deeply on the filling of the Lord in her life for physical as well as spiritual power. He's never let her down.

Living Under His Influence

Dr. Harold Fickett shares the following pattern for how we can respond to the challenge of Ephesians 5:18—to be filled with the Spirit:

Aspire to be controlled by the Spirit of God—Romans 8:5,30.

Acknowledge your sin and receive cleansing—Psalm 66:18.

Abandon yourself to His purposes for you—Romans 9:23-24.

Ask the Holy Spirit to fill you—James 4:2.

Accept by faith the fact of His filling—Colossians 2:6.[2]

Let's re-read Ephesians 5:18 *(NIV)*: "Do not get drunk on wine, which leads to debauchery. Instead, be filled with the Spirit." The word *filled*—to be filled with the Spirit of God—means to be *entirely under the influence of God's Spirit*. Do not be under the influence of wine, strong drink or anything else that clouds and confuses the impact of God in your life.

Do you remember that we mentioned earlier, in our experience at the children's home, that the contents of the vessel had an impact on the vessel—through absorption, creating a scum or warming or cooling the vessel? But the opposite is also true. The vessel influences the contents!

The primary influence in our lives must be God and His Word! But, *under whose influence are you living?* Are you being influenced by your emotional responses—your feelings and your unstable reactions to stress? Is your behavior controlled by the negative things you have been telling yourself, instead of the *truth* of God's Word?

Battling the Negative Influences

Judy had put herself down for years. In the office, she was clumsy and was always blamed for everything. She had nearly convinced herself that she would never be noticed for a promotion, and if she did, she would fail and have to suffer the humiliation of being fired. Yes, she was unable to succeed in anything and it probably had to do with her mousy appearance. She had lived a long time 'under the influence' of the false information that she was worthless, unloved and unappreciated. Her behavior was controlled by this misinformation.

If you want to be God's chosen vessel you must assume responsibility to sift out the false influences and submit to the controlling influence of God's truth.

Believe it or not, *you are not the world's worst mother!*

You have not done the unforgiveable!

The truth is, He remembers you are dust, and while you were still a sinner He redeemed you with His own precious blood.

Some are influenced by the lie that we can do everything right given the right job, husband or circumstances. That sort of lie is equally dangerous! The truth is this: we cannot depend on ourselves, our education, our profession, our marriage, or belief in ourselves—but we *can* depend on God.

He is willing to live His life through you. He will use your personality, your abilities, your circumstances and your gifts, to do what Romans 9:23-24 (*TLB*) says: "And he has a right to take others such as ourselves, who have been made for pouring the riches of His glory into, whether we are Jews or Gentiles, and to be kind to us so that everyone can see how very great his glory is."

Imagine that! We can be vessels for God to pour His glory into!

Some of us are under the influence of the what ifs of our lives:

What if—my husband gets sick of me!

What if—my children don't choose the right way!

What if—I lose my job, am in an accident or find a lump in my breast? Job certainly had more cause than most of us to fall victim to that line of thinking and that negative imagination seemed to have made his difficult situation even worse: "What I feared has come upon me" (Job 3:25, *NIV*). Can you ask the Lord to free you from the influence of these vain thoughts and be filled with His love and peace?

"Cathy" is one of my favorite comic strips. A recent edition went something like this: In the first picture she and boyfriend Max are seated at a candlelit table engaged in deep conversation. Max comments that "We spent the first 18 years of our lives with them."

Cathy replies, "I know, Max. They shaped us, guided us and they gave us our whole perspective on the world."

Max continues to reflect, "And now we do all we can to deny that we're still influenced by them."

Puzzled, Cathy asks, "Max, are we talking about our parents or our TV sets?"

Television has become the greatest influence on our society we are told. How important it is to sift out the negative influence of television without discounting the positive impact it can have.

Jeremiah was feeling sorry for himself. He did not appreciate the hurt and the pain and the negative responses of the people to his warnings. He cried out to the Lord and reminded God that it was for His sake that he was suffering. The climax was his declaration that God had failed him, God had not been there when He was needed!

"The Lord replied: 'Stop this foolishness and talk some sense! Only if you return to trusting me will I let you continue as my spokesman. You are to influence *them,* not let them influence *you!*'" (Jer. 15:19, *TLB*).

What a truth! By trusting God, we are given the opportunity to be *influencers*—not the *influencees*. When we are filled to the brim with Him, we find our joy in being poured out, filled up again and poured out—exhibiting the glory of God.

> So whoever cleanses himself [from what is ignoble and unclean]—who separates himself from contact with contaminating and corrupting influences—will [then himself] be a vessel set apart *and* useful for honorable *and* noble purposes, consecrated and profitable to the Master, fit *and* ready for any good work (2 Tim. 2:21, *AMP*).

Truth-Filled Vessels

What is God's opinion of you? What does He say about you?

In Jeremiah 31:3: _____

_____

In Isaiah 43:1-2,4: _____

_____

In Lamentations 3:22-23: _____

_____

In Romans 8:38-39: _____

_____

In 1 John 3:1: _____

_____

In Romans 9:23-24: _____

_____

And in all the blessings that are yours in Ephesians 1:3-14.

Broken Vessels

David cried out in Psalm 31:12 *(NIV)*, "I have become like broken pottery." He felt useless and cast aside. But there's good news! Even broken vessels can be of use.

In homes in Bible times these pieces of broken vessels, called sherds, were used to carry live coals. Sherds carried warmth, perhaps from a neighbor's fire, to rekindle a spark. Sherds are broken, ill-shaped and have nothing in themselves to be proud of—but they carry live coals!

In many of our churches there are those women whose lives have been broken or damaged either with or without any action or decision on their own parts. Often they feel that they can never be used again. How good it is to bask in the restorative grace of God. If you are that person or have the opportunity to minister to some broken vessels, take heart! God isn't finished with you yet and He delights in using broken things. It is often our own judgmental attitudes that keep those whose lives have been broken from enjoying a new usefulness.

But don't you be a breaker! Lives, as vessels, are fragile and we need to take care to treat each other carefully.

Vessels of Service

When God instructed Moses to build the Tabernacle, He gave definite commands about the furnishings and the vessels to be used in the holy place. They were to be set apart, never used for anything else and sanctified for holy purposes. This is the highest form of usefulness for a vessel. And to think we can, by faith, be prepared for this!

"Take the anointing oil and anoint the tabernacle and everything in it; consecrate it and all its furnishings, and it will be holy. Then anoint the altar of burnt offering and all its utensils; consecrate the altar, and it will be most holy. Anoint the basin and its stand and consecrate them" (Exod. 40:9-11, *NIV*).

Oil in the Scriptures is always a type of the Holy Spirit. How were the vessels used for special service to be made holy? By anointing with oil. They were to be kept for high and holy services. Never to be used for common tasks.

Pompous King Belshazzar gave a great banquet for 1,000 of his nobles. While drinking his wine he gave orders to have golden goblets brought to the banquet. They were the sanctified goblets from the Temple in Jerusalem. They were valuable to captive Israelites beyond any understanding of the drunken king of Babylon or his cohorts.

Daniel was called in to interpret Belshazzar's vision of the writing on the wall. With great courage and supernatural power, Daniel dared to tell the king that God had judged him, and part of that judgment was because he had desecrated the vessels from the Temple.

Vessels of service are not to be used for common things. "If you stay away from sin you will be like one of these dishes made of purest gold—the very best in the house—so that Christ himself can use you for his highest purposes" (2 Tim. 2:21, *TLB*).

You and I can choose to be set apart for service. May nothing less be satisfactory. If God has chosen you for His service, then make sure your life is kept clean. Never allow Satan to dupe you into thinking you can take part in common things. Be a vessel for service in the house of the Lord.

Lord, how can I a chosen vessel be, to bear
    Thy name to others far and near—
That precious message carried, Lord, by me,
    An earthen vessel, frail and full of fear?
Lord, what if this weak vessel e'er should
    break,
Leaving someone without a taste of Thee?
"I know," said He, "that thou art frail to bear
    the message I have put within thy soul.
But nothing that is handled with great care is
    broken, though it be a fragile bowl.
I chose thee not for any strength of thine;
But thou art in My hand, O child of mine."[3]

A PRAYERFUL MINISTRY

As a vessel you are set apart for special service. One of the highest and holiest services we can give is that of prayer.

My suggestion is that you first examine your own prayer life before beginning a ministry in prayer. Are you on intimate speaking terms with your Father in heaven?

Some wonderful books on prayer have been written and excellent helps provided. A simple prayer pattern is probably not new or unfamiliar to you, but I give it again because it might well be the basis for your own life as well as for an intercessory ministry.

Prayer Pattern

The acts of prayer might include these four areas:

A—Adoration or worship. Read Psalm 34:1 and exalt His name.
C—Confession. Read Psalm 66:18 and look into your heart.
T—Thanksgiving. Read Psalm 92:1 and remember, it is a good thing to give thanks unto the Lord!
S—Supplication. Read Philippians 4:6 and talk with God about your needs.

As you go to the Lord in prayer, *go worshipfully.* Consider spending a few moments simply acknowledging God for who He is. Worship Him in the beauty of the Scripture. Read back to your Father the words of Psalm 103, which is a list of all He can be to you.

Include a time of confession in your personal prayer. Confess first all known sin. The Holy Spirit is faithful to let us know those areas of need when we pray, "Search me, O God, and know my heart; test me and know my anxious thoughts. See if there is any offensive way in me, and lead me in the way everlasting" (Ps. 139:23-24, *NIV*).

Do not carry guilt. God intends that we keep short accounts with Him. Realize that just as quickly as you confess your sin, forgiveness is yours. Why are we slow to appropriate His grace in forgiveness? Be a vessel who knows victory in prayer because you have been both willing and able to release your guilt to your Saviour who has already paid for it!

My friend was sharing some frustration with me about a certain loved one of hers—her son. She said that she has always taught her children that they should not partake in the elements of the communion table if they were not up-to-the-minute with the Lord. So, my friend's son became careless and declined to take the elements. Finally this chosen-vessel friend of mine confronted her son with the good news that forgiveness is instantaneous—just as soon as we confess and express a desire for that forgiveness we are forgiven. Sin is not a condition you have to live with; you can know freedom from guilt right now. Sometimes it is more comfortable to co-exist with a few faults than to assume the responsibility that only freedom and holy living afford.

Now, *thank the Lord in everything.* Be careful not to thank God *for* everything—there is so much sin and sorrow around us that He is not responsible for. But thank Him for His faithfulness in the midst of the trial, and for His promises for the future. Thank Him for His peace in the storm. Thank Him for all those conveniences that more than meet your need for more time.

As you come to the Lord with your requests, it is a good idea to have a list of those needs and persons for which you are responsible to pray. A point of frustration for leaders who want to pray for those with whom they serve and those whom they lead, is the impossibility of praying for *everyone every day.* Divide the list and pray for just a portion of those needs each day. Missionaries, church members, neighbors, leaders of our nation and communities need our prayers. Better to pray for fewer each day and to pray in depth.

In his very special booklet called *Manna in the Morning,* Stephen Olford cites the system for remembering special needs that he and his wife use:

Monday: *M* is for missionaries.

Tuesday: *T* is for thanksgiving—that's when we give the Lord the special thanks for wonderful answers to prayer.

Wednesday: *W* is for workers.

Thursday: *T* is for tasks—our job at the church, the ministry that God has given to us.

Friday: *F* is for our families.

Saturday: *S* is for the saints—and especially young Christians, that Christ may be formed in them.

Sunday: *S* is for sinners and in particular, the gospel services for which we are responsible.[4]

🏵 Personal Prayer Time

Write out your own prayer including each of these elements:

Adoration:

Confession: I agree with you God, that _____ is sin and I ask you to forgive me.

Thanksgiving:

Supplication: Lord, I have a special need for _____, in Jesus' name.

The vessel whose abilities are simply . . .

AVAIL	—	ability
USE	—	ability
ADAPT	—	ability
RESPONS	—	ability

. . . is a vessel meant for the Master's use.
Consider the vessel molded, filled and willing to be poured out in intercession.

Praying with Others

Get involved in praying with others! Here are some guidelines for forming a prayer chain, as suggested by Evelyn Christensen's United Prayer Ministries in Minneapolis.[5]

How do you start? Get together with one or two other mature prayers and seek God's will. His will may be for you to pray together for a while before enlarging the group. If you're starting a church prayer group or chain, make sure you have the blessing of your pastor and that he agrees to help if you need guidance. If he doesn't agree, go back and pray for God's timing.

How many members? Keep your group or chain small. There is more chance of each person participating this way. If it grows large, break into small groups or chains.

What about rules? Have specific rules and leaders who are mature Christians and can enforce them.

    a. Start at a specific time and end on time (see 1 Cor. 14:40).

    b. Keep a watch on confidences shared (see Ps. 141:3).

    c. Emphasize the need for private, daily prayer (see John 15:7).

    d. Live cleansed lives (see 1 John 1:9).

    e. Decide what time and how many requests should go through the chain each day. Too many will exhaust prayers.

    f. Pray requests, not answers.

    g. Keep a list of your requests and answers for encouragement.

    h. Meet together for times of sharing and getting acquainted.

    i. Be honest! When problems arise or even if you see one coming, talk to your leader about it. Don't let bitterness begin (see Heb. 12:15).

    j. Be sure to spend time praising—even if you don't see the answers to your prayers at the time (see Ps. 92:1,2).

    k. Be sure to put on the full armor of God! (see Eph. 6:11-18).

Pray for Others

Get involved in intercession! A couple of weeks ago, Rosella, one of my most faithful prayer partners, wrote me one

more of her encouraging notes and enclosed the following article. She asked me if I would like to be prayed for according to
this Scripture. I responded quickly with a resounding yes! It is
an article by Sarah Gudschinsky, a longtime missionary with the
Wycliffe Bible Translators.

In Colossians 1:9-13, *KJV*—"For this cause we also, since
the day we heard it, do not cease to pray for you, and to desire
that ye might be filled with the knowledge of his will in all wisdom and spiritual understanding: that ye might walk worthy of
the Lord unto all pleasing, being fruitful in every good work, and
increasing in the knowledge of God; Strengthened with all
might, according to his glorious power, unto all patience and
longsuffering with joyfulness; giving thanks unto the Father,
which hath made us meet to be partakers of the inheritance of
the saints in light: who hath delivered us from the power of darkness, and hath translated us into the kingdom of his dear Son."

Lord, bless Charles . . . and bless the Gregersons, and bless
Marge, and bless . . .

This is the tenth of June, and custom demands that I pray for
my fellow workers listed on 'Day 10' of the prayer directory. I
don't know very many of these people personally, and I don't
have any news, so my prayer is dry and hurried and impersonal—bless the Grubers, and bless . . . wait a minute!

The next name on the list is my own. And I wonder with
shock and horror if others today are praying . . . and bless Sarah
and bless Shirley . . . and . . . not really praying for me at all.

The apostle Paul lived in a time of poor communication and
lack of news. He carried a heavy prayer burden for churches and
individuals. Yet I have no impression that his prayer was hurried
or dry. It occurs to me that if I use Scripture as a base for my
prayer, it may become more meaningful—more like the prayer I
need from others.

I think I'll try it with Colossians 1.

Lord, fill Charles with a knowledge of Thy will. May he have
Thy point of view in all things. Keep him from decisions made for
self-advantage or according to the perverted standards of this
world.

Give him wisdom and spiritual understanding. Deliver him
from a dependence on the dishonesty and craftiness of man's

wisdom, from conceit and pride. Grant to him the wisdom which is from above—pure, teachable, humble.

Grant that he might bring credit to Thy name and please Thee in all things. Enable him for this not only in his praying and witnessing, but also in the drudgeries of daily living. May small maintenance jobs, errands run, meals eaten, the way he dresses and all else please Thee.

Make him fruitful in good works. Keep him from any self-centeredness or even work-centeredness that would keep him from acts of kindness and goodness and generosity.

Increase his knowledge of Thee. May he see Thee clearly in Thy Word, may he fellowship with Thee in prayer and meditation, may he be so filled with the Spirit of holiness that he may see Thee in truth.

Strengthen him with all Thy glorious power—the power that raised Christ from the dead. Take his weakness and inability that it might be lost in the ocean depths of Thine own omnipotence.

Teach him patience and long-suffering. Make him patient with the shortcomings and irritating habits of his co-workers, in all the daily annoyance and friction. Make him patient in the multitude of interruptions to the problem that he has laid out. Give him long-suffering in the unreasonable upsets and delays which slow the work. And grant to him patience with himself, with his own faults and weakness.

Fill his heart with overflowing joy. May he see Thy overruling love and mercy in every circumstance. May he rejoice in opportunities to show forth the patience and meekness that come from Thee.

Praise be unto Thee, O Lord our God, that Thou hast made Charles to be fit to be a partaker of the inheritance of the saints of light. I thank Thee for Thy mercy and transforming power in his life.

I thank Thee for calling him out of the domain of darkness and into the kingdom of Thy dear Son. I pray that Thou wouldst make the deliverance from darkness and sin a practical reality in his daily life. Bring him quickly to conviction and repentance when he falls into sin.

And may all glory be unto Jesus our Lord and Saviour whose is the preeminence in all things. Amen."[6]

Creative Praying

If you are reading this while alone, why not take this moment to go and fill your vessel with some hot coffee or tea, and then think creatively with me about some ways to have a prayer ministry. All set? Here are seven ideas:

1. *Pray through your Christmas cards!* My dear mother and daddy gave and received hundreds of Christmas cards each year. At their retirement they decided to expand their prayer ministry. As November and December arrived each year, so did the cards. They were collected in a large, attractive basket. At the first of the new year, two cards were drawn daily and the senders are prayed for in Mom and Daddy's morning devotions. Then Mom wrote a postcard to those prayed for with a note of encouragement. The cards were special ones that said "We have prayed for you today" and are still available through Good News Publishers, 9825 W. Roosevelt Rd., Westchester, IL 60153. Attractive prayer postcards are also available through The American Tract Society, P.O. Box 402003, Garland, TX 75040.

2. *Prayer partners.* Four years ago I realized through a friend's suggestion that my own ministry would be enriched through the sharing of concerns with prayer partners. I wrote a note to 31 women friends, mostly from our home church, and invited them to become a partner in believing prayer with me one day each month. Each of them said yes. I made a list and assigned each of them one day and committed myself to pray for each lady on her day. About once a quarter I send a letter to each of my—now 62—prayer partners and give them my schedule, as well as share some of the answers received. Many of them write to me to let me know how to pray specifically for them. How the Lord has blessed us all. If each reader were to set up her own network, just think about the prayer support God's women across the land would supply for His work!

3. *Day Starter.* This is an idea the Lord gave to encourage both new Christians as well as help those "older" ones to begin the day with the Lord.

    a. Phone a partner at an agreed upon time—same time each

day until further notice. Let her call you the second week.
b. Set oven timer for three minutes.
c. First minute will be to share a prayer request or a report of praise.
d. Second minute is to read five or six verses of Scripture. It is good to read through a book of the Bible together.
e. Either one or both of you pray for the last minute.
Hang up as the bell rings!

At the end of the first month, try it again with either the same partner or another. Simply enjoy the encouragement and discipline!

4. *Key 16.* There are 16 elected government officials who have a direct impact on the life of you and your family. The Scripture teaches that we are to pray for those in authority. One way of doing that is to make a list of the names of those 16 elected officials and make it a special prayer list. It might take some research on your part to come up with them, but perhaps it is time you get acquainted with those whose decisions affect you and yours.

U.S. Government (Five) President
                   Vice-President
                   Senator
                   Senator
                   Congressman
State Government (Five) Governor
                   Lt. Governor
                   Attorney General
                   State Senator
                   Assemblyman
Local Government (Six) Mayor
                   City Councilman
                   City Attorney
                   School Board Member
                   County Supervisor
                   Sheriff

Why not, at least occasionally, write a letter to these people to indicate that you are praying for them. It just might make their day!

5. *Make a devotional booklet.* Ask your prayer partners or members of your prayer group or circle to write a prayer, psalm or short meditation. They could be typed and instant-printed or copied attractively. Then each contributor could use her copy of the composite booklet as her prayer guide for Advent or Lent or some other special period of time. The same idea could be used for family devotions. Several families could prepare their own prayers and then assemble a booklet.

6. *Directed Prayer.* This is an idea for leading prayer in larger groups. This method of leading prayer seems to accomplish two special things: (1) it allows for maximum participation without any one person or persuasion to monopolize the entire prayer time; (2) the leader both opens and closes the prayer time, so there is a control.

The leader begins by giving simple instructions: "We are going to pray together, in small groups. Form groups of four or five." If your people are seated around tables make certain that the group will be able to hear one another or divide your groups again. If they are seated in rows, invite every other row to turn around so that they can pray in circles rather than rows.

"We are going to pray together for several subjects. I will give you the topic and then will ask one or two of you in each group to pray briefly—just a sentence or two—for that subject, then I will give the next topic. After a few minutes of prayer I will conclude with prayer."

Depending on the size and purpose of your gathering, you might want to recruit a prayer hostess for each table or location. Also you might want to have prayer lists already available for prayer leaders or even for all in attendance. Consider having each small group spend two or three minutes getting acquainted and compiling their own prayer list, allowing those needs to be prayed for during the last few minutes of your prayer time before you conclude.

Exchanging name tags within groups for further prayer partnerships is another way of confirming the time spent together.

7. *Put it in a basket!* This idea was born out of necessity. A special outreach women's meeting—Spice of Life—was flour-

ishing. However, the prayer time was becoming a drag! Many of the women attending were not accustomed to either lengthy or public prayer. Some of the leaders felt that prayer was a necessary part of the meeting, but didn't know how to control it. The ladies coming had special needs, including the need to be noticed and affirmed—is there any among us who do not have that need! Listen a minute to what was happening:

"Good morning, ladies. We are glad to have a few minutes to spend in prayer together. Are there any requests today?

"My nephew has a broken ankle in Fort Worth. My sister, his mother, has had to leave work to take care of him and her vacation time is already spent. If her husband would help her more she would not have to take valuable time off work to keep her home together. Will you pray that my sister and brother-in-law work this out and that my nephew will heal so that he can get back to his paper route, and . . . and . . . ad infinitum."

"All right, we will pray for that. Did you all remember those names? Are there others?"

"Our dog is lost—son—husband—." "The screen door—neighbors." "Dissension—and on and on."

You have been in meetings like this one, haven't you? The prayer time was taking over! And the ladies were uncomfortable not only with the lengthy and often irrelevant prayer requests, but with the necessary time spent in praying for each one.

Here is how the problem was wonderfully solved:

a. Small attractive baskets were already on the tables for offering, along with welcome packets. Several slips of paper were included.

b. The leader suggested that anyone with a special prayer request write it on one of the slips of paper. Women could sign it if they liked and include their phone number if they wanted someone to call to encourage or pray over the telephone.

c. In a few minutes the prayer request slips were collected in a basket and prayer was offered for them generally.

d. Those who were willing to pray raised their hands, the basket was passed and they each drew a slip to take home for the week.

It works!

✿ What If . . .

If we had to pray by telephone,
 the number we would dial would be at least ten digits
 long.
But first, we'd have to find a phone.
 We couldn't pray while driving—or picnicking.
 At church, perhaps, we'd need to stand in line to
 take our turn.
And what if, when we'd dial God—we got that "busy
 tone?"
 Or even a recording for a disconnected phone?
Or what if one of His angels answered, "Heaven here;
 please hold!"
Oh, think, if when we called we found that God was on
 another line—
 A brother's prayer was being heard at that particular
 time.
We might leave a message; He could call us back some-
 day.
Yes, if we had to pray by telephone, it would be a terri-
 ble thing,
 to dial and dial, be put on hold,
 leave messages . . .
But wait.
Let's see!
 Do I ever make it as hard as that
 For God to get in touch with me?[7]

It was a lovely surprise—yet not really a surprise—a few
Christmas seasons ago, for each of our family members to open
gifts from our daughter Lois. She had carefully packed and
wrapped each one. It was evident that many sessions of her
sophomore ceramics class had been spent in making pots of various shapes and sizes for her Christmas list. Each of them has
her name scratched into the clay before firing.

To the average person, their use might not even be obvious.
But, to me—to us—they were immediately placed in the trea-

sure category! We know the maker and these vessels were chosen with us in mind.

Is that what God has done for you? Is He shaping you, sometimes firing you, filling you—and then presenting you to a thirsty world? He has marked you and set you apart for service. Those Temple vessels were never used for the mundane. Theirs was the highest and holiest of purposes. Is that true of your life? Do not get entangled in trivia!

A chosen vessel was Amy Carmichael. Though she went to heaven in 1951 after spending most of her life working in Southern India, her life and writing continue to impact the world for Jesus' sake. Her volumes of letters to her co-workers and spiritual children give insights into the depth of her constant praying and her continuing conversations with her Lord. Perhaps they endure because of Amy's teenage confession of what her value system would be:

Nothing is important save that which is eternal.

Women, let us be done with lesser things and concentrate on that which is eternal by investing our lives in intercession and in serving others by leading them to a deeper fellowship with the Master Potter.

🏵 Make a Prayer Reminder Magnet

1. Cut out the Scripture and color with felt pens.
2. Cut a bit of cardboard about ½-inch larger all around than the Scripture clipping.
3. Cover with calico or other pretty fabric, glueing in place.
4. Glue the Scripture in center of card, and affix about one inch of magnetic tape on back.
5. *Remember to pray with faith!*

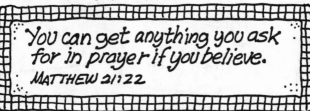

You can get anything you ask for in prayer if you believe.
MATTHEW 21:22

SOME CHILDREN'S
Letters to God

Dear Lord,
   How do I know that you hear my prayers?
   Could you please give me a sign like leaving me a $10 bill under my pillow.
            Gloria
            Age 10
            Forest Park

Dear Lord,
   I say my prayers 3 times a day because I don't want to take any chances.
         Sincerely,
         Mike
         Age 7
         Philadelphia

Dear Lord,
   How many angels are there in heaven? I would like to be the first kid in my class to know the answer.
            Norma
            Age 8
            Dubuque

How to Pray for Your Missionaries

In Romans 15:30-32
- for physical protection
- for an acceptable ministry to the saints
- for journeying mercies
- for divine guidance
- for spiritual and physical refreshing

In 2 Corinthians 1:8,11
- for relief from pressure
- for help in trouble

In Ephesians 6:19
- for God's message for each occasion
- for God's boldness to preach that message

In Colossians 4:3-4
- for opportunities to preach
- for ability to take advantage of the opportunities

In 1 Thessalonians 5:25
- for fellow missionaries, national pastors, national Christians

In 2 Thessalonians 3:1-2
- for liberty in preaching the Word
- for results from preaching the Word
- for the protection of the converts[8]

Prayer Portraits from the Scripture

Discover the situation for these prayers, their petitions and God's answers:

1. *Joshua*—Joshua 7:6-9
   a.
   b.
   c.

2. *Hannah*—1 Samuel 1 and 2
   a.
   b.
   c.

3. *Solomon*—1 Kings 8:22-44
   a.
   b.
   c.
4. *David*—Psalm 51
   a.
   b.
   c.
5. *Nehemiah*—Nehemiah 1:5-11 and 2:4
   a.
   b.
   c.
6. *Paul*—Colossians 1:9 12
   a.
   b.
   c.

✿ Lord, Teach Us to Pray

Scripture Reference: Luke 11:1-10

Please read this portion and make some notes in response to the following questions:

vv. 1-4:

1. What things do we learn about God from these verses?

   _____

   _____

2. What does it mean to pray, "Hallowed be Thy Name"?

   _____

3. On the basis of what we've learned about God, what should be our attitude toward Him when we pray? _____

   _____

4. Why do we need to pray, "Thy kingdom come"? _____

_____

5. Put in your own words, "Thy will be done, as in heaven, so in earth." What difference would this make in the world around us if this were *sincerely* prayed? What difference would it make in your own life? _____

_____

_____

6. What areas of our lives are covered by the next three petitions?

_____

7. How can we, who live in the midst of prosperity pray, "Give us this day our daily bread?" _____

_____

8. Why do you think Jesus attached a condition-to-be-met on the petition for forgiveness? What does an unforgiving attitude do to us personally, both psychologically and physically, as well as spiritually? _____

_____

9. Explain in your own words why the last petition is important.

_____

vv. 5-10:
10. In this parable, what is Jesus trying to tell us about the nature of prayer? _____

11. How important is it to pray specifically? _____

_____

12. Can you identify the attributes of God that Jesus is revealing in this parable? _____

13. Jesus gives us an assurance to pray-ers in both of these parables. What is it? _____

A
Prayer
Promise—Psalm 145:18 _____

_____

Have thine own way, Lord! Have Thine own way!
    Thou art the Potter, I am the clay.
    Mold me and make me after Thy will
    While I am waiting, yielded and still.

Have Thine own way, Lord! Have Thine own way!
    Hold o'er my being absolute sway
    Fill with Thy Spirit 'til all shall see
    Christ only, always living in me![9]

Look, You're a Servant!

MEET THE LORD'S SERVANT

> And the Lord's servant must not quarrel; instead, he must be kind to everyone, able to teach, not resentful (2 Tim. 2:24, *NIV*).

"It's a great summer job, Daisy. Besides, where else can you make that kind of money and still go to the beach everyday?"

A college friend talked me into taking a summer job at a large hotel on the Atlantic Coast, waiting on tables. Of course, there were a few details she neglected to include, like the fact that the base salary would just about cover a beach pass and a hot dog or two on the boardwalk occasionally. And another thing—servants' quarters in the hotel were five flights up and I shared my room, right under the hot tin roof, with 15 or 20 other waitresses!

Our employer believed that the low salary would encourage us to do our job so well, and to be so alert and available, that we could retire early on our tips. But I have a problem with this—is the customer then responsible for the servant's salary or is the employer? Oh well, the summer flew by and despite all of our complaining, we returned to college as brown and chubby as could be.

Now, when David and I are enjoying pie and coffee in a restaurant, we sometimes evaluate the service and discuss the amount of the tip. Invariably my husband, who forgets how many times he has given me this morsel of information, will ask me, "Do you know what tip *really* means?" Playing dumb, I bite and he recites, "To Insure Promptness, that's what it means!" Then we proceed to dig into our pockets and come up with what we think our waitress's promptness deserves. A silly game and yet we are part of a society that seems to insure rewards for service.

Scripture's Servant Is Obedient

God has His own system and invites us to live by this system with a fresh newness in all we do and think. Tips help, to be sure, but God is interested in a glad spirit, willing hands and a servant heart.

Remember right from the beginning: The Scripture's pattern for leadership is in becoming a servant of the Living God!

Life can never be dull again
When once you've thrown the window open wide
And seen the great world that lies outside—
And said to yourself this wondrous thing:
"I'm wanted for the service of the King!"[1]

The picture of a bond servant occurs often in Scripture. A slave served his master out of obligation. Sometimes the master would choose to free the slave. Then it was up to the slave to decide whether or not he wanted to continue to serve his master. If he chose to do so, he became a bond servant and wore a mark that indicated his status.

Whom do you serve?

Why do you serve?

* * *

A finely dressed nobleman passed the slave auction block and heard the auctioneer shouting the merits of the strong, robust, dejected slave being sold. The man began to bid, higher and higher, and to the surprise of the onlookers, soon found himself the owner of the slave.

He paid for his purchase and quickly proceeded to loosen the bonds, saying with pity, "Take off the chains; I have bought you to free you! Go!"

The slave threw himself at the master's feet and cried out,

"Please let me serve you for the rest of my life. Let me be your slave, by love!"

* * *

Are the following verses, learned by many of us during our childhoods, too simplistic for the complicated ministries in our lives?:

> "Serve one another in love" (Gal. 5:13, *NIV*).
> "Now the most important thing about a servant is that he does just what his master tells him to" (1 Cor. 4:2, *TLB*).

It *is* inconvenient to be a servant and is often uncomfortable—but always worth it.

> Can you see how dealing gracefully with interruptions requires a servant heart?
> Can you see how to find purpose and meaning in routine requires a servant heart?
> Can you see how assuming the risky role of leadership requires a servant heart?
> There is so little in our present worldly society that encourages the attitude of willing service to others. So what has conditioned you in your life to be willing to serve?

> Take my life, and let it be
> Consecrated, Lord, to Thee;
> Take my moments and my days,
> Let them flow in ceaseless praise.[2]

Let's look at the servant's characteristics. Where are your strengths?

A Servant Is Willing to Serve

A true love slave serves with gladness. When Isaiah was touched by God with the vision of live coals cleansing and sanctifying him—and then was challenged to serve and witness—his response was clear, "Here am I. Send me!" (See Isa. 6:8.)

An executive for a major airline once said that their greatest problem was finding men and women who were willing to serve. Everyone wanted to lead but no one wanted to serve.

Since serving is the scriptural way—and if we want to serve gladly and not under protest—let's go one more time to the altar for another touch of the live coal.

Both the title and the contents of a current book trouble me. *Our Struggle to Serve* is a collection of the experiences of several gifted Christian women as they have struggled to find their place in the ministry of Jesus Christ. Is it a struggle to serve Christ or is it a struggle to submit to the servant's role? Women, even in the Body of Christ and in His established Church, are being bombarded with pressures to assert their rights. Some struggle who are not designed for this to be involved in church leadership in congregations and denominations. There is so much work to be done and so much serving. Please, ladies, let's get on with it! A love slave gives up her rights in order to fulfill her responsibilities.

A Servant Is Unselfish

Another paradox in serving is demonstrated in the Golden Rule: you do for others what you wish others would do for you. When you are tired or discouraged or tempted to self-pity, pick yourself up, dust yourself off and learn to live by Jesus' service ethic. What do you need from others? Loyalty? Give yourself loyally to Christ and those around you as never before! Do you need encouragement? (Wow, do *I* need encouragement!) Then sit yourself down and write at least three notes to encourage others. Do you need some attention or affirmation? Begin to think like Christ. Do what Jesus would do and phone someone who is seldom recognized.

As I write these words I see on my wall, among other significant signs, mottoes and photos, a message specially framed: "Ask not what your mother can do for you, ask what you can do for your mother." Most of our kids have no idea about the Golden Rule at home, do they? Will someone tell them about how much we need affirmation and service, especially service behind our own front door?

A Servant Has a Submissive Spirit

"And all of you serve each other with humble spirits, for God gives special blessings to those who are humble" (1 Pet. 5:5, *TLB*).

> I'll go where you want me to go, dear Lord,
>   real service is what I desire.
> I'll sing a solo any time, dear Lord.
>   but don't ask me to sing in the choir.
> I'll do what you want me to do dear Lord,
> I like to see things come to pass.
> But don't ask me to teach boys and girls, O Lord.
> I'd rather just stay in my class.
> I'll do what you want me to do, dear Lord,
> I yearn for Thy kingdom to thrive.
> I'll give you my nickels and dimes, dear Lord.
> But please don't ask me to tithe.[3]

What has conditioned you in your life to be willing to serve? Very little, if anything, in our present society encourages the attitude of willing service to others. Jesus has a different idea! He challenges the follower of the Way, Truth and Life to be great by serving. It is the way to be first, for those who are at the "top" spiritually are to be responsible for serving the people at the "bottom."

The Servant's Menu of Characteristics
Part 1

---

1. Ephesians 6:5: _____

_____

2. Matthew 6:24: _____

   _____

3. 1 Peter 5:15: _____

   _____

4. Luke 9:24: _____

   _____

5. 1 Corinthians 4:2: _____

   _____

6. Mark 10:42-45: _____

   _____

Servant-Leadership Has Its Price

My friend Joyce is the choir director in her middle-sized church. We were having lunch together recently and talked about this book along with some of her great ideas for her expanding choir program for the fall.

"Be sure to tell about some of the things a servant-leader is *not* allowed to do. I've learned some of them the hard way. Some might be just for choir directors, but I think they'll apply to any leadership position." Here is Joyce's list:

1. The servant-leader is not allowed to have excuses, like headaches, dentist appointments or a lack of funds.
2. The servant-leader is not allowed to celebrate birthday celebrations or anniversaries that land on scheduled meeting nights.
3. The servant-leader is not allowed to attend her children's program at school if it conflicts with anything having to do with the committee. (In Joyce's case half the choir can

leave after going over the Introit twice in order to be on time to see the school awards program but the director must stay at her post!)

4. The servant-leader is not allowed to disagree with anyone who has a better suggestion.
5. The servant-leader is not allowed to be disgusted or to react negatively to a lack of courtesy on the part of any committee member.
6. The servant-leader must pick up on dropped responsibilities even though they have been delegated.

Does this sound at all familiar? Don't you sometimes wonder if we have any leaders at all in our churches?

What Would Jesus Do?

It happened in the Upper Room. Peter reacted with embarrassment to Jesus' suggestion that He wanted to wash Peter's dusty feet. How did the others react? Did each of the disciples hope that one of the others would take care of this customary amenity? Did John say, under his breath, "Let James do it—I am tired." Or did Nathanael shoot that look across the room that spoke louder than any words, indicating that it was about time Matthew got down off his high horse and started serving?

However it happened, it was Jesus Himself who took the basin and towel and served while saying, "I have set you an example that you should do as I have done for you . . . . No servant is greater than his master . . . . Now that you know these things, you will be blessed if you do them" (John 13:15-17, *NIV*).

If ever there lived one who could have said, "Do as I say," it was the Lord of glory. Instead, He gently exhorted, "Do as I do."

* * *

It was only the pastor's third Sunday in his new church. He told the worshipers that he had wanted to bring a wash basin and a towel and place both in the front of the sanctuary by the pulpit. But he could only find a chipped enamel bowl in the kitchen and besides, a kitchen towel in the front of the church might raise a few eyebrows. He decided against it.

"Anyway," he said, "if I'd done with that basin and towel what Jesus did, we would have all felt a little uncomfortable. And if I had gone down to you high school boys on the third row and asked you to take off your shoes so that I could wash your feet, I'm not sure which of us would have been the most uncomfortable—you or me. Perhaps that same hesitancy is felt as we move out into the dailiness of our lives between Sundays. Many of us feel inept at using a basin and towel, whether we are being served or are serving in humility."

He confronted the congregation with the strong words of Jesus, "Do as I do!" None of us left that service, I am certain, without the conviction of the Spirit of God upon us to become servants, in a basin and towel ministry.

Nearly one hundred years ago Charles Sheldon wrote *In His Steps,* a novel based on a series of his sermons. Since the lessons still need to be learned, the book's popularity has survived and it has been reprinted many, many times.

The story opens with the Reverend Henry Maxwell speaking carefully to his congregation. "I want volunteers from First Church who will pledge themselves, earnestly and honestly, for an entire year, not to do anything without first asking, 'What would Jesus do?'"[4] Those four words became a commitment to a changing life-style. And the story line is the unfolding of the effects on the town, its businesses and its people by the simple application and forethought of what Christ Himself would have done in any given situation.

There is so much in the Scripture that lets us know what Jesus would do. Jesus would not defend His own reputation when criticized unjustly, would not waste time and energy in self-justification or take popularity polls about His leadership. Jesus would not harbor resentment when others disappointed Him and would not indulge in comparisons of levels of commitment.

"Your attitude should be the same as that of Christ Jesus: Who, being in very nature God, did not consider equality with God something to be grasped, but made himself nothing, taking the very nature of a servant, being made in human likeness" (Phil. 2:5-7, *NIV*).

Another example is Philip. In the book of Acts we read that

some changes had to be made organizationally in the fellowship of believers. There was some complaining by the Grecian Jews against the native Hebrews that their widows were not being given their rightful supply of food. So a committee meeting was held and a serving committee was chosen. These were to be waiters—servants—and the qualifications were high for waiting on tables! They were to be full of the Spirit of God and wisdom.

Is this not in keeping with the scriptural principles of greatness and leadership?

"Whoever Wishes to Be Great" is the title of an article by Dr. Howard Hendricks for *Worldwide Challenge* magazine. He gives this insight:

> Philip, the great evangelist, also got his start serving tables. Perhaps it was his experience in serving people that made him sensitive to the voice of God. When the Spirit came to him in Samaria, telling him to go down into the desert, Philip didn't say, "Lord, I'm a metropolitan man, I've got a big city-wide campaign going here. I don't specialize in those desert experiences."
>
> He knew that if God were calling the shots, he couldn't lose. And it is altogether possible that the Ethiopian he led to Christ became the man who opened the whole continent of Africa to the gospel in the first century.
>
> My friends, you shouldn't gripe if God has you serving tables. Who knows, you could be in training for evangelism. God could have you serving tables now to prepare you for a far greater ministry later.[5]

The Servant's Menu of Characteristics
Part 2

1. Read John 13:4-17. Who is the one who assumed the task of washing the feet of the others? List some things you could do today that would exemplify this attitude to those in your own family.

2. Read Acts 6:1-6. What were the qualifications for the servants recruited in this passage?

> For who is greater, the one who is at the table or the one who serves? Is it not the one who is at the table? But I am among you as one who serves (Luke 22:27, *NIV*).

The Eternal Tips

The Lord may ask a lot of His servants but the rewards cannot be compared: "I confer on you a kingdom, just as my Father conferred one on me, so that you may eat and drink at my table in my kingdom and sit on thrones" (Luke 22:29-30, *NIV*).

I for one don't want to miss it! Hand me a basin and towel—or my tray and apron!

There is another kind of reward for service pictured in Matthew, in the parable of the talents. Do you remember that the talents were distributed, and the one with the least dug a hole and buried his? The next invested his and gained five more. But the one to whom the most was given did well! He made the biggest investment and realized the most returns for the Master. So, what was his reward? A vacation? A bonus? No! It was more work, more responsibility and a wider sphere of service. "You have been faithful with a few things; I will put you in charge of many things" (Matt. 25:21, *NIV*).

Can that be translated, "You have done so well with the visiting plan for this nursing home that I will allow you to coordinate the schedule and program for all five that our church is responsible for each month"? Or, "How well you have been working on the kitchen committee! Since you know where everything is, you can now plan the annual women's luncheon for 300 in May!"

Count on it—God has more for you in mind.

Take my love; my Lord, I pour at thy feet its treasure store;
Take myself, and I will be ever, only, all for Thee.[6]

❀ The Servant's Reward

1. Read Acts 8:26-39. Philip had started waiting on tables and could have easily rebelled at the new area of service. Instead, he ministered to one and possibly opened up the entire continent of Africa to the gospel in the first century. How was he rewarded?
2. Read Philemon, vv. 10-17. Onesimus means _____ _____. Is that a reward? What reward is Paul asking for Onesimus, now that he is a Christian?
3. Read Matthew 25:21. What is the reward of a faithful servant? Are you prepared?
4. Read Luke 22:25-30. What does Jesus say the servant can look forward to? How does Jesus characterize His ministry on earth?

SERVE WITH STYLE

We wait on *tables*. We set *tables*. We read time*tables*. We *table* the discussion. We decorate the *tables*.

Never underestimate the power of the *table*! But how does this fit in our service?

Tables are for meeting around. There is something non-threatening in having a table between.

Tables are for getting acquainted. A fellowship group is immediately established for sharing, for praying, for discussion.

Tables are involving. Each one around the table is included. There's no back row!

Tables are convenient. A good place to put your notebook, craft project or coffee cup.

Tables are for refreshments. Even a snack at your get-togethers is enjoyable.

Tables can be stages. The decorations can serve as a stage on which to illustrate visual ideas, center on a given theme and confirm the desired truth.

Try Imaginative Place Mats

1. A place mat can be a *puzzlemat.*
   Put your icebreaker or get-acquainted puzzle on your mat and have it copied on brightly colored paper.
2. A place mat can be a *program.*
   The outline of your event, even the songs, can be attractively and conveniently placed in front of each participant.
3. A place mat can be a *prayer list* or a *newssheet.*
   Use it as a vehicle for announcements, garage sales, missionaries' addresses, clever quotes or cartoons.

Bulletin covers are readily available at your local Christian bookstore. Often they have small amounts left over in an edition (50-100) which can be purchased at a fraction of the original cost. The bulletin covers most often have a Scripture on them and a colorful picture which can be the cue for other table decorations. Their $8\frac{1}{2} \times 11$-inch size makes the perfect placemat for a coffee fellowship or a dessert table.

The following is a pattern and instructions for a special place mat that one women's group used to prepare for a denominational luncheon to serve over 1,000! Each mat was of course unique and served as a take-home gift for each guest. The women also made many extras which were sold so others (like me!) went away with enough to dress up their own family table.

🦋 Directions for Making Quilted Placemats

Cut 32 triangles from good quality cotton prints carefully (this is very important to get a good finished product). Be sure to place bottom of triangle on straight of cloth. Before you begin to sew them together, lay them out as you want them arranged in the finished mat to form the most attractive pattern.

Sew a strip of seven across, making sure the bottom of the triangle is the *straight* of the fabric. Next sew two strips of nine triangles, then another of seven. Press each strip carefully, then sew them together. Press the whole piece. Cut the back of plain fabric (permapress unbleached muslin is best), and a piece of white flannel or blanket sheeting for middle layer, a little larger than the pieced mat. Put the three pieces together and baste with large machine stitches around the edges. Run some basting stitches *by hand* across in several places to hold the three pieces together. Then quilt with small even stitches. Do *not* quilt with machine. Trim edges and apply bias tape around the edges to finish.

An easy way to cut triangles

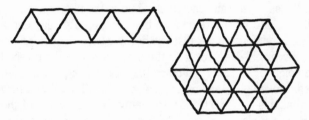

Preparing Tables of Forgiveness

Most women enjoy setting a table, for an attractive table adds much warmth and festivity to a luncheon or dinner. That added touch can change an atmosphere and create a happy eating environment.

A prepared table may also have significance in the life of a Christian. A few summers ago I guided a Thursday night Bible Study series, attended by a number of new Christians. The group's eagerness to search the Scriptures was a challenge.

Some time previously God had begun to show me how preparing a table could be used to reach an unbeliever or to build bridges to those who need to be reconciled to others and to God. I suggested to this study group that there are times in the life of a Christian when he might literally prepare a table to ask forgiveness of a friend or a loved one. When a person has injured a fellow Christian or borne a false witness, for example, there are matters which must be cleared up. And the Scripture says, "If we confess our sins, he is faithful and just and will forgive us our sins and purify us from all unrighteousness" (1 John 1:9,

NIV). Often a table is that precise effort that one makes to talk it over and make things right—first with the person involved and then with the Lord.

I was careful to make clear that the "prepared table" idea was my own personal observation. However, God had used it in my life. One of the new Christians, a vivacious blonde named Jill, was quick to tell me that she did not like the idea of preparing a table to make things right. Everyone smiled at her honesty and then proceeded with the study.

The next Thursday night Jill was bursting with excitement and asked if she could share what God had done in her home that week. We all agreed and she bounded up to the platform.

Jill told of how the telephone had rung on Tuesday and a neighbor had informed her that she had started a petition to ban Jill's five-year-old daughter from the neighborhood. She listened as the neighbor violently ran down the child, telling of trampled pansies, broken glass and other incidents. As Jill wondered how to combat this lady next door, suddenly the discussion of the past week's Bible study came to her mind and she decided to prepare a table for this woman. When the neighbor paused to breathe, my friend invited her over to discuss the terrible five-year-old. The neighbor said, "With pleasure" and hung up.

Quickly Jill placed a cloth on the coffee table with two tea-cups and some cut flowers and set the tea kettle to boiling. She put the cream and sugar down just as the doorbell rang. In walked the livid neighbor, but when she saw the table, she responded, "Oh, I'm sorry, you're having company." "No," replied Jill, "I thought we could have coffee and discuss my daughter." Jill prayed for God's wisdom as she asked the blessing and, when she opened her eyes, she saw her neighbor crying. "It's not *your* daughter, it's *mine*," the neighbor blurted. "Why I lashed out at you, I'll never know, but I can't cope with my children, my husband or my home!"

With this admission Jill started sharing Christ.

* * *

I shared this story at some meetings in Texas. A lady wrote and said it had touched her life in an unbelievable way. She and her husband had wronged many people and they made up their minds to start preparing tables for the ones they had wronged. In her letter she related that in one week, they had held four dinner parties to apologize, to make things right and to settle past hurts. She said the joy of the Lord was flooding their home in a new way. However, at the end of her letter she asked for prayer. They had made a list and realized that it would take four months of using this method to mend matters with all the people they had hurt or cheated. But they were happy to have started the process.

I encourage you to search your heart. Possibly you need to prepare a different kind of table. This too, can change a hostile atmosphere into unbelievable peace and create an environment in which Christ will work in one's life.

"As the offering began, singing to the Lord began also" (2 Chron. 29:27, *NIV*). That's His promise for tomorrow's women![7]

But Remember, I Don't Do Windows!

The very word *volunteer* suggests a willingness to serve, a choice and a volitional act. I am available!

Face it, the needs are there and often women in the Church are just the ones who see them!

After all, they live next door to troubled families, to grieving individuals, to discouraged parents, to lonely widows and to convalescents.

You want to serve and to volunteer your skills, but how do you go about it? You look to the Church and perhaps you see that your church is either unable to meet certain needs or seems otherwise occupied.

It is my considered opinion that women in churches are over-challenged and under-enabled! In other words, we are told to visit the sick and the imprisoned, clothe those in need, feed the hungry and comfort the grieving. But are we expected to go on to the street corner to advertise our availability or to look in the Yellow Pages for some names and addresses of the needy?

Are *you* the volunteer your church has been waiting for to organize a car pool to take some cheer to the county old folks' home? Or to offer your garage for a food deposit for those who will need food resources for the winter months? Or to spearhead the hot line organization for the Crisis Pregnancy Center? Most often, ministries in and through churches are only limited by the lack of willing volunteers.

Jesus made no vague comment regarding our responsibility to do for others what we have allowed or expected the government to do. His instruction to "do unto the least of these as unto me" (see Matt 25:40) carried with it the judgment for those who don't!

The Lord has a sense of humor, don't you think? In a certain county close to home here in Northern California, the Lord has called upon the volunteer forces of the church in a unique way. For years, church members have been praying for the lost on foreign soil; praying that the Lord would raise up volunteers to minister. They have faithfully packed missionary barrels, written to and prayed for their missionaries.

A few years ago, the Lord began setting up an entire Asian community with the influx into one particular county of something over 60,000 Asians! Then came a good-sized Hispanic community and it numbered in the tens of thousands. It was as if the Lord was saying, "I am bringing the mission field *to* you. Now, let us see if you are as willing to volunteer to take a Vietnamese mother grocery shopping or to teach English to a small group of Hispanics!"

I was recently informed that through the Los Angeles port alone, over 5,000 immigrants and refugees arrived *monthly*. The Lord is bringing the opportunity to our own doorsteps. Call your church office for ideas based upon requests they have received. Call your local Salvation Army office for ways you can help. Call the local jail, juvenile hall or prison. Call a Pro-Life organization for information on how you can help. You undoubtedly have lots of ideas of your own. Perhaps you need to be the servant-leader of the volunteer group from your church, the enabler instead of the challenger!

This kind of voluntary service requires more than a willingness. It requires initiative, often persistence and usually the flexibility of inconvenience. But you see, we have not been called to convenience. We've been called to serve and it might involve doing windows or even floors!

❀ A Special Poem for Volunteers

Many will be shocked to find, when the day of judgment nears,

That there is a special place in heaven set aside for volunteers,

Furnished with big recliners, satin couches and footstools,

Where there is no committee chairman, no group leaders or car pools.

No eager team that needs a coach, no bazaar and no bake sale.

There will be nothing to staple, not one thing to fold or mail.

Telephone lists will be outlawed, but a finger snap will bring

Cool drinks and gourmet dinners—rare feasts for queen and king.

You ask, "Who will serve these privileged few, and work for all they're worth?"

Why, all those who reaped the benefits and not once volunteered on earth![8]

Some Ideas from 2 Timothy 2

VOLUNTEER to serve by . . .

Speaking and sharing in a nursing home or devotional meeting
like a TEACHER

Writing to your legislators or becoming part of a Crisis Pregnancy Hotline
like a SOLDIER

Discipling a young Christian or sponsoring an athletic team for ministry
like an ATHLETE

Serving as a Committee Chairwoman (volunteers are particularly hard to find—like a needle in a haystack—for Chairwoman
like a FARMER

Inviting some lonely neighbors over for coffee and an informal Bible Study

            like a WORKMAN

Organizing a prayer chain for shutins

            like a VESSEL

Offering to plan a guest night banquet for internationals in your community

            like a SERVANT

My own dear dad is in a nursing home in the East. My sisters and I, from four different states, keep in close touch with phone calls, letters and small packages sent often. Daddy has been an "in charge" person all his life and these are difficult days of having to depend wholly on others to have his needs met. Mother went home to heaven just a short time ago and Daddy has been unable to write any notes or letters on his own.

The mailman arrived last week with a letter showing Daddy's return address neatly typed on the corner of the envelope. I opened it quickly and read words of love and encouragement. It was signed with a shaky, "Oceans of love, Daddy." Then the P.S. revealed that it had been typed by a volunteer who was visiting the residents to do some of the things the nurses and other staff members did not have time to do.

Hurray for volunteers!

A Housewife's Lament

Hello, Mrs. Jones, I've just called to say
I'm sorry I cried when you called today.
No I didn't get angry when your call came at 4
Just as the Cub Scouts burst through the door.
It's just that I had such a really full day
I'd baked 8 pies for the PTA.
And washing and ironing and scrubbing the floor
Were chores I had finished not too long before.
The reason I cried and gave that big yelp
Was not 'cause you phoned to ask for my help.
The comment that drove me berserk
Was, "I'm sure you'll have time because you
    don't work!"[9]

HOW TO PLAN A BANQUET WITHOUT MAKING IT A LIFE'S WORK

"Let's have a banquet!"

"Forget it, it's too much trouble!"

"But, we've always had a spring thing, and *everyone* expects it."

"Then, let *them* do it! We've spent hours making favors, flyers and food and only succeeded in losing friends in all our efforts."

"But you have to admit that it *is* a great outreach opportunity."

"You're right, Joan, my neighbor had never been to our church and now she comes regularly to Bible Study."

"Carolyn *did* come up with the cleverest of all possible table decorations. They were phenomenal conversation starters—as if the women needed one—and made fellowship hall look like it never has before. I've heard that she and the gals who met in her home to create them had such a good time laughing and fiddling and gluing, and coffee-ing, that they want to do it again."

"But we are so involved in all the other areas of program—what with Sunday School, preparation for VBS, our Nursing Home visitation and on and on and on—right around the world! How can we get involved in something that seems to produce such limited results?"

* * *

The conversation went on and on—and before the get-together was over, there was a great deal of enthusiasm for having the banquet. But who would be the chairman? Someday I am going to write a book and call it, *Please Let Me Be Chairman*! Because it has been my experience in challenging women to service and ministry, that when a woman is urged by God (often in the form of loving, Christian friends and associates) and takes the creative risk of leadership for a special event, she is more than rewarded and fulfilled to see God use her. If only more would try—and risk—and let God create through her! Why don't you volunteer to chair the banquet?

Here are some steps you might take to make it happen:

1. *Invite women to be part of this special committee.* Let it be a group that meets for this specific project alone. Those who participate will then know the time limit of their involvement. Notice in the chapter on the servant-farmer some guidelines to committee meeting and preparation. Invite a good group to your first meeting, indicating that there will be opportunity for each woman to select her own area of involvement.

2. *Why shall we have the banquet?* Let that be first on your agenda. Too often the event is less than satisfactory because the steering committee is vague in its purpose. Remember the conversation and the comment from one woman that the banquet last year had been an outreach? That is a good reason for having a special event. As a matter of fact, perhaps the best—since more relatives and friends, often unsaved ones, will attend a Mother and Daughter Banquet sooner than most other events. Then, let the goal be outreach—even pure evangelism. You are then able to design the program and setting to encourage fellowship and challenge to accept the love of Jesus personally.

There are other good reasons for having a banquet. Think of some and note them right here:

What might be the banquet goal for the following situations—other than simply to consume a meal or hear a speaker? Remember to choose a big enough, specific and significant enough goal that will make all the work worth it! Perhaps several goals can be realized through the same event.

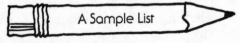

A Sample List

a. Graduation time for students.

b. An influx of neighbors because of an adjoining senior citizens complex.

c. A finish to a community sponsored evangelistic campaign.

d. Your church leadership has contributed a full and productive year of faithful service.

e. An unsung missionary heroine is home on furlough with her husband and four children.

The list can go on and on. Consider your group or church calendar and see if there might be other occasions when there are opportunities available in a banquet setting for fellowship, outreach, education, inspiration, appreciation, etc.

3. *Who will help?* As the chairman, you will want to create an outline, in writing, of the various committees needed. You'll also want to supply simple job descriptions:

a. We need women to create the setting—*decorations*. Be definite as to tables, platform, wall space, color scheme, favors. Each committee member may want to take one of these projects.

b. We need women to create the focus—*program*. After the theme has been selected, the program committee can go to work contacting speakers, coordinating the feature (i.e. demonstration, fashion show, multi-media presentation) with music. They will follow through on thank you notes, honorarium checks, as well as having the final program folder printed.

c. We need women to get the word around—*publicity*. These women will create posters, flyers, bulletin inserts, perhaps a ticket design. Remembering that the single most effective publicity tool is personal invitation, they might want to create a phoning team especially for those on the periphery of the fellowship. Sometimes, the ticket sales and name tags can work under this committee, depending on how many women you have to help.

d. We need women to set the mood—*hostesses and hospitality*. This group recruits at least one hostess per table, who will make certain that those at her table are made to feel welcome, cared for and acquainted with others. The Hospitality Group is sure to have several greeters at the door, enough so that they can circulate guiding the guests to appropriate tables, directing "traffic" and answering questions like, "Where are the rest rooms?" or "Where is the telephone?" or "We need six seats together!"

e. We need women to plan the goodies—*menu and food services.* You will want to determine the guidelines for each group so the jobs do not overlap. For example, does the food services group take responsibility for serving the tables or does that go under hospitality? You will clarify that in a way appropriate to your own group and helpers.

Some questions for consideration:

How many can our church kitchen serve without renting or borrowing plates, cloths, silverware, pans, etc.? What are ways we can budget this meal effectively? Could our women contribute salads? Or desserts? How about trading the cooking and serving with a neighboring church group? Shall we go to a restaurant for a change?

f. We need women to handle the money and budget—*finance.* This group can distribute the tickets and deposit the funds. The Chairman will need to receive the bills and arrange for payment. Sometimes a table can be set up for ticket sales during other occasions in your church. Or reservations can be made by telephone, for payment at the door.

4. *Some things to accomplish at your first meeting:*

a. Try to *find committee chairwomen* and allow everyone to indicate their area of interest. Occasionally, the chairwoman will realize that adjustments must be made outside the group meeting. Please use tact in moving away from discussion of personalities to move the meeting along. This, and other areas of discussion, can be sidetracks to the essentials and even barriers to smooth-running relationships. Bathing your meeting in prayer will help a lot in this regard. Trust God to help you to affirm each one and let your personal enthusiasm help others to sense the joy of serving.

b. *Set the calendar* for each meeting of the general committee. Suggest that the subcommittees meet between these times. The general or steering committee will consist of each of the chairwomen of the subcommittees outlined above. This will allow you to efficiently use your time and resources in planning. Make each committee meeting a report session, setting the tone as leader, that you respect each person's ability to accept and follow through on their own responsibility. Don't let your time together deteriorate into discussion groups!

c. *Select a theme* for your banquet. Three are suggested here in this chapter but have everyone come with some other ideas gathered beforehand. Remember your goals and select a theme appropriate to the fulfillment of those goals—but make it a graphic one—one that suggests decorations, a color scheme and even a program idea. Make the theme one that is easily visualized and it will be simpler for your committees to work.

d. *Do something creative* to motivate the women! Select a theme—even a poster with the theme printed on it. Let your imagination be your guide:

Anchors Aweigh
I Remember When
Through the Looking Glass
The Sky's the Limit
Queen for a Day
Sugar and Spice

Give each of the women an assignment to one of the necessary committees for the banquet, excluding perhaps the finance. Divide them into small groups. Using the selected theme, let them plan the banquet right there in 10-minute buzz groups. Perhaps one or two of the situations suggested under point two will help to answer the why of the banquet you are planning. The report time for this short exercise is exciting—exhilarating—encouraging!

You can do it! It will happen—to God's glory!

```
Banquet Idea 1
I Remember Mama or Memories Are Made of This
```

DECORATIONS: Green patchwork tablecloths with antiques placed in groupings on tables and piano, etc.

Often women are willing to decorate their own table by bringing some articles from their own homes, including a tablecloth and napkins. This theme allows especially for individuality in decoration. Use these possibilities. Sometimes an antique shop is willing to set up a display, even sharing some of the background of an article or two.

NAME TAGS: Use the shape of something old like a high-button shoe, etc.

PROGRAMS: Old newsprint gift wrap, store wrapping paper or even wallpaper samples. Try to find the sepia or brown tinted kind.

ALTERNATE CENTERPIECES: Hurricane candleholders made from clay pigeons glued together with a glass chimney, candle and ribbon. Complete directions are also available in *Life with Spice Resource Manual,* p. 40.

ATMOSPHERE: Memorabilia boxes scattered around the room, or a large memorabilia box (simply arranged by putting together crates or rough wood) filled with old pictures, symbols and miscellaneous items from people's attics. Invite all who are coming to bring along an article which holds a special significant memory for them. Let them take time to share these with the women around their tables.

MESSAGE: Look at the lives of women in the Bible and note that for which they are remembered. Or consider some women in our history, and recall what our heritage is through them. Missionary women, unsung heroines of the church are good examples. Go to the library and find the book, *Mama's Bank Account* by Kathryn Forbes. It's the story of a Norwegian family whose mama really made memories!

Grandmother's Perfect Day

Grandmother on a winter's day
Milked the cows and fed them hay,
Slopped the hogs, saddled the mule,
And got the children off to school.
Did a washing, mopped the floors,
Washed the windows and did some chores,
Cooked a dish of home-dried fruit,
Pressed her husband's Sunday suit,
Swept the parlor, made the bed,
Baked a dozen loaves of bread,
Split some firewood, and lugged it in
Enough to fill the kitchen bin.
Cleaned the lamps and put in oil
Stewed some apples she thought might spoil.
Churned the butter, baked a cake,
Then exclaimed, "For mercy's sake
The calves have got out of the pen."
Went out, and chased them in again.
Gathered the eggs and locked the stable
Back to the house and set the table.
Cooked a supper that was delicious
And afterwards washed all the dishes.
Fed the cat and sprinkled the clothes,
Mended a basket full of hose,
Then opened the organ and began to play
"When You Come to the End of a Perfect Day."[10]

Banquet Idea 2
The Bread of Life or Give Us This Day Our Daily Bread

OCCASION: Ladies' brunch or banquet; a missionary dinner with an emphasis on sharing the Bread of Life with others.

DECORATIONS: Brown and white checkered tablecloths with yellow accents. Centerpieces of bread dough baskets or bread of life dough on breadboards. Or, varnished bread loaves tied with gingham ribbon and decorated with strawflowers set on breadboards. Use varnished bagels for candleholders. (To make varnished bread, bake an unsliced loaf four to six hours or two days in a pilot-lit oven. Varnish with at least two coats.)

PROGRAMS: Yellow or tan breadboards tied with brown ribbon. Make name tags to match. Perhaps use recipe cards for programs—including a bread recipe.

FAVORS: Miniature bread-dough baskets lined with muffin paper filled with nuts and mints. Or two or three small breadsticks tied up together by a checkered ribbon—with Scripture verse and program attached.

FEATURES: Have a demonstration of bread dough art. You might even have a Baggie holding a little bit of salt clay at each place and allow the women to try their hand at shaping some dough to take home and bake. Get everyone involved! Or, have a skit of grandmothers sharing some of their breadmaking tips.

Try this mathematics problem for an appetizer. Of course you don't make the numbers known until the problem is solved and the prize awarded!

Multiply the number of loaves in the boy's lunch by the number of fishes.	5 × 2
	10
Add the number of disciples Jesus called.	+ 12
	22
Multiply by the number of the bread chapters in John.	× 6
	132
Add how many times Jesus said we are to be willing to forgive.	490 (70 × 7)
	622
Subtract the number of times Jesus said He might fail us.	-000 (Hurray!)
	622
Add the number of people who were miraculously fed on that day on the hillside.	+ 5000
	5,622

Be surprised by your answer! Some loaves of *homemade bread* will be prizes for the correct answer.

MENU: Sandwich loaves with fruit salad. Or a small round loaf of Shepherd's bread for each person, with center scooped out and filled with beef stew. Replace "lid" after trimming off bread so it forms a crust cap.

MUSIC: "Break Thou the Bread of Life," "The Breaking of the Bread" or "Let Us Break Bread Together."

MESSAGE: Use the topic of, "The All-Sufficient Christ," noting John 6, Mark 6:30-44 and other Scriptures.

```
Banquet Idea 3
Portraits by the Master Designer
```

DECORATIONS: Off-white fabric with paint blotches for a design-print. Unbleached muslin could be used as a background for the pieces of art displayed as centerpieces on small easels. Have as many as are willing make contributions to a display of their handwork—from oil paintings and watercolors to hand-designed stationery and decoupage. Create an art festival of praise to the Master Designer!

PROGRAMS: Should be in the shape of an artist's palette. Napkins can be in a folk-painting design or in different solid colors.

FEATURES: Invite a Christian artist to give a demonstration or a chalk art presentation emphasizing the theme of God's handiwork. Someone in smock and beret might set up an easel and lighting to make profile silhouettes—particularly of the little girls. Have women share their original poetry and music. An album of these presentations would be a lovely remembrance of the occasion.

MUSIC: Invite a violinist or a string ensemble to provide music. "Master Designer" would be an appropriate song, as well as "In the Image of God." These are available at your local Christian music supplier or bookstore.

MESSAGE: Psalms 139 provides a beautiful setting for your meditation. Psalms 8 is the creation Psalm and could be shared with a color slide presentation for illustration. Invite the women to contribute one or two slides which could be labeled then assembled to illustrate the Psalm.

THANK YOU!

Taking a breather between planes in a large, impersonal airport, I went to the snack bar for some coffee. There it was, glued on to the cash register: Thank you for letting us serve you. Then, as the agent directed me to the gate, he added, "Thank you for letting us serve you!"

When it happened a third time, I realized how my own attitude was affected. Of course I was paying for their services, but the simple, even hackneyed phrase made me feel special. It is a new wrinkle, don't you think? Somebody, somewhere in that airport had launched a campaign to raise morale—and it worked!

Come to think of it, I had recently bought some shoes and was made to feel that the salesperson was doing me a favor to sell me his wares. This type of experience has been repeated over and over, until the new attitude of appreciation for the privilege of serving is revolutionary!

Louise Henderson is a retired art teacher who now resides in Livermore, California. She's a tiny, creative dynamo with a servant heart that moves and shakes her world with Jesus' love. I was given one of her rock figures painted into a blue-frocked *happy person* as a gift and I wanted to meet the artist. Her home is a beehive of activity—one alcove has rocks and miniatures in cubby holes. Paints, brushes and makeshift palettes are all mixed up with bits of silk flowers and pebbles for trimming. In another corner are slabs of shale that she paints with scenery and often Scripture. Her husband was busy shelling bags and bags of walnuts they had harvested for gift giving.

"Louise, do you suppose you could make me some *happy people* for me to use with our seminars on leadership?"

"Meet me in two weeks and I'll have them for you," she replied.

The unveiling came at a lunch meeting and I do wish you could see them! They're simply charming!

"Louise, tell me more about why you just make *happy people*? Aren't there any other expressions you can create?"

"Daisy, I have served the Lord for years—in Sunday Schools, in women's work and in the public school system. A while back I was just plain tuckered out in the Lord's work. I had spent years, it seemed, trying to get others to serve."

She went on, "I would call up Mildred, and say, 'Mildred, will you please bring some cookies to the VBS planning meeting this week?' and she would answer that she was busy and wouldn't have time before her hair appointment to get them done.

"So I would call Joan or Barbara or Genevieve and ask them to pick up some kids for Awana group or go to the nursing home or help to sort the clothes for the needy families. Everything seemed to stand in their way of serving. Then, I got an idea! It was from the Lord, I'm sure!

"I even do seminars about it now and I call them my Ya Getta principles! Instead of begging people to serve, I call Mildred now and say, 'Good morning, Mildred. Guess what you get to do today for Jesus!' Then I tell her that she gets to bring cookies for VBS. The same goes for Joan or others, 'Here is what you get to do today for Jesus.' It works Daisy, when we begin to realize that it is our privilege to serve Him!"

It is hard for us to imagine that the Lord Jesus does not *need* us—He allows us the opportunity to express our love by serving. He could certainly get the job done without our help, but let's not miss the blessing of cooperating with Him in kingdom building.

Let's make it our prayer:

Dear Lord,
Thank you for letting us serve you.

Amen.

 Choice Menus

Sherbet Punch

Nice to serve at a new member's reception.

    2 pkgs. raspberry Kool Aid
1½ cups sugar
    1 46 oz. can pineapple juice
  46 oz. water
    1 qt. 7-Up
    1 qt. raspberry sherbet, scooped

You can use lime Kool Aid and lime sherbet or orange Kool Aid and orange sherbet, etc. Prepare no more than 15 minutes ahead of time. Serves 20.

Tostada Dip

Use at an Ole! Fiesta for Mexican Missions

1 lg. can refried beans
1 8 oz. carton sour cream
   Cheddar cheese grated finely
1 lg. tomato chopped finely
1 envelope avocado dip mix
2 green onions finely chopped
1 small can sliced olives, drained

   Layer on dish in the order given. Serve with tortilla chips. Serves 8-10.

Pumpkin Pie Cake

Use at a Harvesttime Dessert for senior citizens.

4 eggs, slightly beaten
1 tsp. salt
1 tsp. ginger
1 29 oz. can pumpkin
1½ cups sugar
1 tsp. cinnamon
1-13 oz. can evaporated milk

1 pkg. yellow cake mix
1 cup chopped nuts
1 cup melted butter or margarine
   whipped topping

   Mix together all ingredients in the left-hand column. Pour into a 9 × 13-inch pan. Sprinkle and cover with the cake mix. Top with nuts. Pour melted butter or margarine over entire mixture. Bake at 325 degrees for 1½ hours or until knife comes out clean. Top with whipped cream or Cool Whip. Serves 12-16.

NOTES

Chapter 2
1. Jo Carr and Imogene Sorley, *Bless This Mess* (New York: Pillar Books, 1969), p. 64.
2. Cathy Meeks, *I Want Somebody to Know My Name* (Nashville: Thomas Nelson, Inc. 1978).
3. Mark Hatfield, "Excellence: The Christian Standard," *World Aflame,* April 1978, p. 5.
4. John W. Gardner, "Excellence! The Christian Standard," *World Aflame,* April 1, 1978, p. 5.
5. Leroy Eims, *Be the Leader You Were Meant to Be* (Wheaton, IL: Victor Books, 1975), p. 50.

Chapter 3
1. Sheldon Vanauken, *A Severe Mercy* (New York: Bantam Books, 1979).
2. Barbara Johnson, *Where Does a Mother Go to Resign?* (Minneapolis: Bethany Fellowship, Inc., 1979). Used by permission.
3. Author unknown.
4. For helpful and creative teaching tools, may I suggest you read *Innovations,* a magazine published five times a year by the David C. Cook Publishing Company.
5. This lesson was inspired by Edith Schaeffer, "Christians Are Singing People," *Christianity Today,* July 1, 1977.
6. Author unknown. Taken from: *Uncle Ben's Quotebook.* Copyright © 1976. Harvest House Publishers, Eugene, OR 97402. Used by permission.

Chapter 4
1. Adapted from Simeon Stylites.
2. Sabine Baring-Gould, "Onward, Christian Soldiers."
3. Frances R. Havergal, "Who Is on the Lord's Side?"
4. George Duffield, Jr., "Stand Up, Stand Up for Jesus."
5. Frances R. Havergal, "True-hearted, Whole-hearted."
6. As told by Elizabeth Elliott.
7. Author unknown.
8. William Booth, "I'll Fight."

Chapter 5
1. *Strategy for Living* by Edward R. Dayton and Ted W. Engstrom. © Copyright 1976, Regal Books, Ventura, CA 93006. Used by permission.
2. This particular chorus is just one of many such choruses written by an old general of The Salvation Army. It can be found in *The Salvation Army Songbook* (New York: Salvation Army Supplies and Printing, n.d.), p. 478.
3. Printed by permission of the author Naomi Taylor Wright, author of *An Ever-Widening Circle,* seminar speaker and Bible teacher.
4. Rev. James Braga, source unknown.
5. From: I'M RUNNING TO WIN
   By: Ann Kiemel © 1980 Used by permission Tyndale House Publishers, Inc.
6. Ibid.
7. Taken from *SPIRITUAL FITNESS* by Mini Jane Johnson. Copyright © 1973 by The Zondervan Corporation. Used by permission.

Chapter 6
1. *Autobiography of God* by Lloyd John Ogilvie. © Copyright 1979, Regal Books, Ventura, CA 93006. Used by permission.
2. Ibid., pp. 57-58.
3. Ibid., pp. 58-59.
4. Ibid., p. 62.
5. Charlotte Hale Allen, *Power Magazine,* 1979.
6. Flora Larsson, "Weeds and Flowers," *Just a Minute, Lord*

(Wheaton, IL: Harold Shaw, 1974), p. 43.

7. Dr. E. Stanley Jones, source unknown.

8. Author unknown.

9. Flora Larsson, "Hoeing," *Just a Minute, Lord* (Wheaton, IL: Harold Shaw, 1974), p. 75.

10. Robert Schuller, source unknown.

11. Author unknown.

Chapter 7

1. Author unknown.

2. Daisy Hepburn, *Why Doesn't Somebody Do Something?* (Wheaton, IL: Victor Books, 1980), p. 87.

3. John Stott, *Guard the Gospel* (Downers Grove, IL: Inter-Varsity Press, 1973), pp. 67-68.

4. Ethel Barrett, *Don't Look Now—But Your Personality Is Showing* (Ventura, CA: Regal Books, 1968), p. 44.

5. E.E. Hewitt, "More About Jesus", public domain.

6. Author unknown.

7. Adapted from *News and Views*—Business Women's Class, Highland Park Baptist Church, Chattanooga, TN.

8. Author unknown.

9. Author unknown.

10. Amy Carmichael, *If* (Fort Washington, PA: Christian Literature Crusade, 1966). Used by permission.

11. Katherine Sorensen.

Chapter 8

1. Author unknown.

2. From a sermon by Harold L. Fickett, Jr.

3. Author unknown.

4. Stephen F. Olford, *Manna in the Morning* (Chicago: Moody Press, no date).

5. Adapted from United Prayer Ministries.

6. Sarah Gudschinsky, from a tract published by Wycliffe Bible Translators.

7. Diane Ower, source known.

8. Author unknown, from Focus on Missions.

9. Adalaide A. Pollard, "Have Thine Own Way, Lord" in *Worship and Service Hymnal* (Chicago: Hope Publishing Co., 1907).

Chapter 9
1. Author unknown.
2. Frances R. Havergal, "Take My Life."
3. Author unknown.
4. Charles M. Sheldon, *In His Steps* (Grand Rapids, MI: Baker Book House, 1978).
5. Howard Hendricks, "Whoever Wishes to Be Great," *Worldwide Challenge*.
6. Havergal, "Take My Life." Public domain.
7. Author unknown.
8. Author unknown.
9. Author unknown.

The Popular *Life with Spice* Bible Study Series by Daisy Hepburn

Notes

Notes

Notes

Notes